Praise for

Welcome to the Real World

"Lauren is one of the brightest and most passionate and articulate young leaders out there today, inspiring a whole generation of young women to take their careers into their own hands. Girls, do whatever Lauren says! Immediately! You won't regret it!"

—Randi Zuckerberg, founder and CEO of Zuckerberg Media

"Lauren Berger has written the book we all wish we had when beginning our careers. *Welcome to the Real World* is a practical, funny, and inspiring crash course in tackling your first job, and proves it's possible to kick butt right from the start."

—Kate White, author of *I Shouldn't Be Telling You This: How to Ask for the Money, Snag the Promotion, and Create the Career You Deserve*

"Lauren Berger is the big sister you've always dreamed of having. *Welcome to the Real World* offers concrete tips on how to turn your passion into your purpose. If you're at a turning point in your life or career, then this book is for you!"

—Gabrielle Bernstein, *New York Times* bestselling author of *May Cause Miracles*

"Lauren's book is practical and comprehensive . . . and so needed."

—Nancy Lublin, CEO, DoSomething.org

"Succeeding in this economy requires savvy, guts, and flexibility. Lauren's advice is spot-on."

—Jason Feifer, *Fast Company*

WELCOME TO THE
REAL WORLD

ALSO BY LAUREN BERGER

All Work, No Pay: Finding an Internship,
Building a Résumé, Making Connections,
and Gaining Job Experience

WELCOME TO THE

REAL WORLD

FINDING YOUR PLACE, PERFECTING YOUR WORK, AND TURNING YOUR JOB INTO YOUR DREAM CAREER

LAUREN BERGER

HARPER
BUSINESS

An Imprint of HarperCollins*Publishers*
www.harpercollins.com

HarperCollins books may be purchased for educational, business, or sales promotional use. For information, please e-mail the Special Markets Department at SPsales@harpercollins.com.

FIRST EDITION

Designed by Renato Stanisic

Library of Congress Cataloging-in-Publication Data has been applied for.

ISBN 978-0-06-230730-9

14 15 16 17 18   OV/RRD   10 9 8 7 6 5 4 3 2 1

This book is dedicated in loving memory to Justin Syden. In December 2013, Justin would have graduated from my alma mater, the University of Central Florida, to embark on his own adventure into the real world. The way he lived his life inspires me every day.

Contents

Acknowledgments

In the acknowledgments section of my first book, I thanked all the people who told me no, as they made me prove myself day after day. Now I'd like to thank the people who told me yes. Because of your belief in my brand and in my company, I've been able to share my message with the world and encourage young people to be proactive and make things happen in their own lives.

This book represents the beginning of the next chapter in my journey. I'm excited to face the challenges that come along with any new endeavor, to advocate for my ideas, and fight for what I believe in. I look forward to continuing to lead this army of inspirational young people who are entering the real world. They are quite a force, so get ready.

Mom and Dad

Someone recently asked me what's behind my success. The answer was simple: Failure wasn't an option. My parents made sure of that. They raised my brother and me to strive for success and because of their constant belief in us, regardless of the paths we chose, it worked. Thank you for instilling your confidence, work ethic, and love in both of us. We are great because of you.

Jonathan

My little brother has turned into quite the businessman. Although he's across the country living his New York City life, I try to insert myself into the equation, as much as possible. One day, I'll convince him to come and run my business. I couldn't be more proud of the young man he's become.

Mike

Behind the scenes there's a special guy who is the center of my real world. He helped out so much with this project—editing pages, fixing computers, and going on late night coffee runs. I can't wait to see what the future brings.

My Los Angeles Family

This book is about the real world and my real world started eight years ago with Lauren Gold, Shannon Howard, Lauren Tully, and Rob Forman, when we all moved to Los Angeles after graduating from college. Although we all do different things in our careers, we've had the privilege of growing up together, figuring things out together, and really becoming a family of our own. When your real families are across the country, close friends are even more important. Looking back, I can't imagine a real world without them.

My Friends

I'm the kind of person who only has close friends. I've known most of them for more than ten years. These people live all across the country and provide me with constant love and support on the daily. To all of you, thank you.

My Book Team

Years ago, I emailed fifty book agents looking for representation. Forty-nine of them said no. Katie Kotchman said yes. Now, Katie still supports me, even when I pitch her the craziest ideas. I'm lucky to have her on my team.

You always hope that people see your work and it speaks to them. I want to thank Colleen Lawrie from HarperCollins for believing in my project right off the bat and working with me every step of the way.

My Intern Queen Team

I wouldn't have been able to carve out time to work on this project without the help of several people. I want to thank my agents, brand coordinator, interns, and ambassadors for all of their help with this process.

My #InternQueenFamily has been there with me since day one. I want to thank all of the young people who have been a part of our Intern Queen community throughout the years. Watching you all succeed inspired me to write this book. I'm so happy to continue our conversation and talk with you about your first, second, and third jobs.

My First Boss

And lastly, I want to thank my very first boss (you know who you are) for showing me that you can have everything—you just need to work hard every single day for it. You will always be the person who paved the way and showed me that I could do anything.

Introduction: The Start of Something

I think today is Tuesday . . .

Lately, the days seem to blend together. Do I sound wasted? I'm not, I promise. Two weeks ago, I started my first job at the largest talent agency in the world. I'm in my cubicle, sitting Indian style on my swivel chair. There are no windows. I stare at the white walls all day long. I drive to and from work in the dark. Each day, I'm exposed to new processes and personalities. My capacity for new information expired days ago. People keep telling me they have "high expectations" for me, but what does that even mean? I feel like my life isn't mine.

On my first day, everyone was *so* nice. But overnight, it seems, those same people have turned short and snippy. My boss is clearly getting over her honeymoon stage with me, and has started to freely express her opinion of my work—and it's not so great. It's only been two weeks and my world has been completely flipped upside down. The girl who was supposed to train me started working for a managing partner within the company so she now has no time.

My daily tasks include scheduling my boss's meetings; planning a European vacation for her and her husband; sending her clients new movie scripts; keeping track of the call sheet; and answering the phone, which rings every two seconds. I just have too many things in front of me. I don't know where to start. I'm lost in a paper zoo with to-do lists, highlighted scripts, half-written letters, crumpled receipts, and unused napkins everywhere. Beneath the papers are boxes of unopened gifts, designer handbags, food cartons, organizers that aren't being used for organizing, and Sharpies in every color. Do I really need another to-do list? Before I can get to work, I hear my boss yelling my name from her office. And trust me, I'm not the only one who can hear her. She sounds angry . . . but for some reason, I still haven't moved. What did I do this time? I've already dropped several phone calls, double-booked three meetings, e-mailed a script to the wrong client, and heated up my boss's frozen lunch in the plastic container it came in, which *apparently* means I gave her cancer. Or maybe she meant the microwaved container would give her cancer? Who knows.

I'm glued to my seat. Finally, I take a deep breath and drag my feet into my boss's office. "Lauren! Why don't you have a pen and paper? Do you not take your role here seriously? You should ALWAYS be taking notes!"

My head is spinning. I don't say anything. I pivot, turn back to my desk, grab an old memo pad and pen, and circle back into her office. "Hello, again," I say dryly, forcing a no-teeth smile. She rolls her eyes.

"We have a problem, Lauren. Look around. Tell me what the problem is."

I look around her office. It's a new office. We just moved into a new building. It has a big window and a large desk. Definitely an upgrade from the last building. "What's wrong?" I ask, looking around at her new office apprehensively. "Well Lauren," she's going somewhere with this and I know it's not going to be good. "I don't have any furniture in my office. If you took a walk around the floor, you would notice that every other agent has new furniture. Some have couches, chaise lounges, others have tables, and some have nice chairs, but I have *nothing* in my office. I'm the only agent in the office with *no furniture* which is weird because I asked you to order office furniture for me *weeks* ago. You were supposed to get it here by Monday."

My stomach drops. Uh oh. She is right. We spoke about it. I didn't do it. I don't know why. It wasn't on purpose, I just didn't do it. It must have been written on a piece of paper somewhere in my paper zoo. I'm clearly not organized enough and just don't have my work life together. I apologize and go back to my desk to order the furniture. Ugh.

....

WELCOME TO MY REAL WORLD. This is it. This is the big glamorous life of a second assistant to a movie star talent agent. I feel like such an idiot. I'm THAT assistant—the one who can't do anything right. Other assistants feel better about themselves because they know they don't mess up as much as I do. Honestly, I know I could get fired at any moment. And the worst part is my boss is right— everyone is right—I am bad at my job. Me, the girl who had fifteen internships, the girl who was the most prepared job candidate in the world, was terrible at her job.

Meanwhile, my personal life was just as messy. Suddenly, I had about eighty new friends who wanted to hang out all the time. Every weeknight, after leaving the office late, we'd get together for drinks or dinners we could barely afford on our assistants' salaries. We'd get drunk, go to bed, manage to get back into the office at 7 A.M., and then convince someone to order McDonald's to cure our hangovers. Because there were so many of us, every day was someone's birthday, and when there was a birthday there were cupcakes, bagels, or pizza. And because our workloads were so heavy and our days were so draining—we lived for the food.

The weekends were just as busy and chaotic. At night, we went out to ultra-trendy bars, took tequila shots, kissed strangers, and woke up the next morning craving more McDonald's. I was meeting new people, never had a moment to be lonely, and had so many nights for the memory books. Now, let me play Debbie Downer for a moment and explain what wasn't so great about this seemingly cool lifestyle. My body and my brain were always on go: I never had time to stop, I never had time to breathe. It was one thing right into the next. Because of this, I didn't have any time for my family or old friends on the East Coast. Because of the time difference, I hardly spoke to anyone. When I was leaving work, my parents and friends were in bed. When I drove to work in the morning and had time to talk, they were at work. I also had no time for any sort of personal errands; things like going to the bank, the grocery store, and the dry cleaners just never happened. My bills and dirty clothes started to stack up, my car started to break down, and I started eating out every night. All of those birthday parties, free bagels in the break room, and snacks in the afternoon were really starting to affect my body. Working out wasn't an option because I had no time for it. I couldn't excel at my job because I wasn't in control of my job; my job was in control of me. I felt completely hopeless.

I didn't know how to turn things around at work or in my personal life because there was no one to tell me, no one to train me. I needed help and had nowhere to get it. My parents couldn't understand how such a glamorous job could be so bad and would just tell me that it would "get better." *Super* helpful, guys. For someone who was always told that I had so much potential, all of a sudden I felt useless and replaceable.

When I look back at that time, I think, "Wow, what was I doing? And why was I doing it?" I had so much going on but I needed rules. I needed guidance. No one had prepared me for what I was experiencing and it was so frustrating. Why didn't anyone tell me how to prioritize, organize, manage my time, get my work done, build relationships, and take care of myself?

By the time I finally realized things needed to change in my work life, it was too late. The opportunity to be promoted and to move to another department within the company had already passed me by. I had gotten to the point where I was stuck. And it wasn't until I left the agency and started my own business that I was able to realize how many different mistakes I had made. Once I was able to look at the entry-level tasks I did as an assistant from a different perspective, I was able to understand what I *should* have been doing at that job. I had to learn the hard way.

When I launched my own company I decided things were going to be different. I made a list of everything I did wrong at my first job and vowed to learn from my mistakes and improve. I searched deep inside myself to find the power, the motivation, and the courage to adopt a new set of rules. No more playing it safe and trying to just stay caught up. I would stay ahead, learn new systems, perfect my work, become a superstar in my field, and turn my new job into my career. This time, I was ready to conquer the world.

Because of that new mind-set, things changed. Today, I sit here writing this book, only a few years removed from that first job, but it feels like decades have passed. I'm CEO and founder of my own company (www.InternQueen.com). I work from a home office, surrounded by pink notebooks and sparkle pens, and I make the rules. Most important, I don't feel lost, undervalued, or replaceable.

My weekends aren't filled with as many parties, but the friends that I met back then are still with me today and hopefully will be for many years to come. I'm much more organized and put together, and I've learned to think about the consequences of my actions. You won't see me scarfing down cupcakes anymore (at least not too often). I truly believe that the world is mine and I can do anything I want in it.

And I'm not alone. The friends that started with me as assistants are finally starting to get the career successes they've been working so hard for. We all started as entry-level assistants in Hollywood. We knew we wanted success, but we couldn't have described what it was back then. We knew we wanted to make things happen, but we didn't know really what those things were or how to get the ball rolling. We just sort of jumped right in immediately after graduation with no idea of what we were getting ourselves into.

If you had asked me how I felt about my life and career path a few years back, I probably would have told you I was frustrated and anxious. But today, I look back on that time—that precious, dreadful time when I had no clue what was going on—and I smile. Because it was in that time frame, in those moments, that I truly learned who I was, what I wanted to do, how to work, and how to get things done. Yes, I learned through trial and error, but hopefully this book will help you skip some of those errors and become the confident, organized, and successful person I know you can be.

Here I get the opportunity to tell you what no one told me. I get to tell you how bad it can be but also how good it can get. This is information that you need to know before starting your first job. And through my own experience, I can relate to what you are going through. I know what it feels like to hate the daily grind, to feel stuck, to feel like you are bad at your job, and to feel like you're on a slow path to nowhere. But I also know what it feels like on the other side. And most important, I know how to get there. I know how you can change your outlook, mind-set, and the quality of your work. I know how you can challenge yourself every day at work so that you don't lose the passion and motivation that drives you in the first place, and how you can succeed in whatever version of the real world you choose.

You spend approximately 25 percent of your life at work. There are so many books written on how to find and land a job but what about actually keeping a job? What about turning your first job into your dream job? Keys to on-the-job success?

I'm sick of people calling us—the Millennials—lazy, privileged, entitled, or the trophy generation. We've always waited for *our time*, and *our time* is now. Now we shine and show the world the resilience we have inside. This book is the first step. It will give you a path to follow, ideas to think about, and something to aspire to.

Each chapter of this book provides helpful strategies on how to handle and manage different aspects of that first, second, or third job. Those of you who are on your fourth or fifth job will have my next book to look forward to! We begin our adventure with some pillars of success and basic rules that I follow in every work-related situation. One of the most important parts of chapter one is the section on rejection—something our generation often has a difficult time with. Later, I will cover how to do a standout job on common entry-level tasks, and how to organize, prioritize, and maximize your time. I love chapter five because it's all about building and managing relationships inside the workplace. Of course, I include a section on personal branding, using social media to your benefit, and share specific techniques for each social network in terms of managing your presence and your relationships online. In chapter six, "Oops, I Did It Again," I cover common mistakes in the workplace, issues with coworkers and your boss, and how to ask for a raise or a promotion. The last chapters of the book are all about your personal life—as your work life is only half of the battle. It's so important that you understand how to keep yourself balanced as you navigate this crazy time. Organizing your finances isn't fun, but it's absolutely necessary. And going to the gym may interfere with happy hour, but you'll feel so much better if you make it a priority at least once or twice a week.

Once you are done reading this book, you will

- Shift the way you *think* about the workplace and adopt a new set of *rules* to follow for success
- Increase your confidence, determination, and ability to follow through at work
- Think big and execute well every time
- Better organize your work life, desktop, inbox, and mind-set

- Efficiently prioritize your day-to-day tasks
- Properly maximize the time you spend at work
- Successfully create and manage your personal brand at work
- Build lasting relationships with your colleagues and team
- Navigate sticky office situations
- Embrace entrepreneurship regardless of position, rank, or title
- Develop efficient time-management techniques inside and outside the office
- Raise awareness in regard to your personal finances
- Separate your personal life from your work life
- Increase your probability of getting promoted
- Hopefully, take your boss's job (one day)!

Almost all of the subjects I'm discussing here apply to any industry. I've had lengthy and transformative conversations with all kinds of professionals and successful executives in many different industries: Journalism, publicity, publishing, banking, sports, law, and media. We all had similar stories, made the same mistakes, and shared the same laughs. And every single person lamented that they never had a book like this to show them the ropes of the real world.

....

WE ALL HAVE A POINT of origin. A place we credit for our successes and our failures—a place where we become the people we are today. When it comes to our personal lives, it's usually where we grew up or at least the place we call home. When it comes to our professional lives, that place is usually our first job. For some it's at college, for others it's at an internship, but for most it's at our first jobs where we grow up, learn the ropes, make mistakes, and launch our careers.

People sometimes think that because I'm an entrepreneur, traditional career advice never applied to me. They assume that no boss means no rules and no structure. Not true. Without my first job, I wouldn't be where I am today. If I hadn't been able to watch my first boss organize her workload, manage her time, deal with coworkers, contacts, and clients, I'd have no idea how to manage my time, run my day, or proactively excel in running my business. No matter how successful I become I cannot deny the power of that very first job—my miserable, emotional, terrible, magical first job. I grew up at that job, I became a professional at that job, and without that precious first experience, I don't know where I'd be today . . .

Let's talk for a moment about the origin of this book. Once my first book, *All Work, No Pay*, was published, I thought to myself, what's next? I brought myself back to those first years after college and asked, "What did I need the most help with?" Right away, I was stuck on the concept of exploring that first job. Just thinking about that experience made me roll my eyes and chuckle at the same time. In brainstorming the content for this book, I thought about all the different mistakes I made (there were *so* many), everything I would have done differently, and the biggest lessons that I learned over the course of my first job. I kept thinking to myself, "What do you want to tell everyone? How can you help them rock that first job?" I wrote down ideas for days! I have so much ground to cover with all of you, and I'm excited to jump right in.

Your first job, just like life, will be filled with moments of doubt and frustration, but also moments where you feel truly rewarded. As we travel together on this roller coaster, it will be crucial to remember that everyone has his or her own starting point. Everyone has an origin, and I'm here to help you with yours. And so we begin . . .

WELCOME TO THE
REAL WORLD

CHAPTER 1

My Rules for the Workplace

Dear Reader,

I love writing letters. I especially love writing letters to my readers. So before I get started, I want to talk about you for a moment. Over the course of the last few years my real world has come full circle. I started my first brand, www.InternQueen.com, in 2009 and eager, ambitious students from all over the country jumped on the bandwagon. They came to my little internship site every day, applied for new positions, and read my advice on how to make the most of any career-related opportunity. As my brand and company approach our fifth birthday, I'm proud to have watched these young men and women blossom into some of the most qualified, professional young people in the world. I know success is possible because I've experienced it and I've watched so many of these students follow my lead and achieve it themselves. I've watched my network of students graduate college and go on to work at some of the most prestigious companies in the world. They work at media companies like Hearst, Gannett, Rodale, Disney, and Reuters. They work at fashion companies like Rachel Roy and Charlotte Rousse. They work at educational institutions like the University of Kentucky and Ohio State University. They work at advertising and public relations agencies like Jack Morton and Edelman. They work at financial companies like Northwestern Mutual and Citi. They work for sports organizations like the NFL and the Green Bay Packers. They work for Fortune 500 companies like Boeing and Johnson & Johnson.

The proof is in the pudding. They've followed the workplace rules that I'm about to show you and they've found success— regardless of which real world they've chosen. I've spoken to hiring managers in many different industries and asked them to describe the common mistakes that entry-level employees make, and so many of them were the same. A friend and personal trainer at Crunch Fitness Centers shared the same information about his entry-level trainers as another friend who is a store team leader (management role) at Target. My professional contacts at NBC shared the same information as a friend at Bloomberg. It doesn't matter what path you've chosen, these rules and the content of this book will be helpful just the same.

We all have our own version of the real world. Some of you might become entrepreneurs and run your own businesses (like me). Others might find their real worlds defined within the banking, engineering, publishing, or media industries. You might find your real world as a teacher, a nurse, a doctor, a lawyer, or even a lifelong secretary! No matter what that world is these rules will help.

So take a moment, prepare yourself, grab a highlighter or a notebook, and let's run through these rules, this mind-set, these ways of conducting yourself in a professional environment. Enjoy. And re- member, this book is only the beginning of our relationship together. I hope we're in touch for years to come.

Best,
Lauren Berger

You've graduated school. Congratulations! I understand how quickly things are moving. One minute you are bumming around with your roommates after finals, doing a whole bunch of nothing and the next minute you are moving into that new apartment, ready to start day one of that very first job. AHHHHH! I'll scream for you. It's exciting, it's nerve-racking, and it's scary—all at the same time. You walk in on day one and yikes! You have your work cut out for you. You don't know where to begin.

Now remember, success isn't defined by just having any old job that gives you a paycheck. Success means being happy in the way you're spending your time every day. Success is being able to constantly grow and learn, to make mistakes and then pick yourself up the next day.

In this chapter, I've outlined a few keys to success. I'm going to walk you through each concept. We start out discussing the importance of confidence, putting yourself out there, then move on to thinking big, following through on your commitments, thinking about the consequences before making decisions, dealing with rejection, your attitude in the workplace, and how to stay balanced.

This chapter is unique and special to me because I bring you all into my world and show you how I did it and how I do it. This chapter is sort of like my cookbook, filled with recipes on how I've learned to carry myself and think about my work. You never know where these pointers will take you, but hopefully you are able to think about them and integrate them into your own work life. It's important that I introduce these techniques now, as I want you to have them in the back of your mind as you go through the rest of this book. Without these concepts, these characteristics, and these ideas I wouldn't be me and I wouldn't be able to do what I do. Later in the book, I will introduce several experts and recent grads and explain their tips and techniques for success.

RULE 1: CONFIDENCE IS KING

I'm known as the queen and confidence is king. Seriously, your confidence can make you or break you. Confidence should be your best friend. Mine gets me through any situation, whether it's my job, my day, an embarrassing moment, or a truly regrettable moment. Having confidence allows me to get through anything.

Am I the most confident person in the world? No way. I can be jealous, immature, embarrassed, and vulnerable—just like everyone else. I admit, I've been in situations and at fancy parties where everyone will explain what they do (publicist, agent, reporter) and I hesitate before introducing myself, because what I do is so far removed from that world. I start to question things: Do I sound stupid? Why would they care about what I do? I can't necessarily "help" them with anything. Do they need me in their lives?

It's not a good feeling. And we all do this. We spend so much time doubting ourselves and feeling insecure about our skills, our appearance, our goals, our way of getting things done—we just can't seem to find the confidence within ourselves. When I feel like this I tell myself what I've accomplished and how I followed my passion and turned it into a job—a great one! And I'm able to talk myself out of the hole.

Let me give you an example. I took a workout class last week; it's called Piloxing, kickboxing meets Pilates—super LA. The workout room was packed with thirty-five girls dressed in lululemon attire. You know the scene. The only available space for me to stand was in the front and center of the room. A pretty scary and visible place to be, but I didn't care. I took my stance. I proceeded to jump, dance, and box my little heart out until, all of a sudden, I felt like I was going to pass out. I didn't drink enough water. I thought I might fall over. I was a bit embarrassed to have to draw attention to myself, but the other option was falling over, which would have been way worse. I walked out of the classroom, had some water, felt better, and walked back in, head held high. I rejoined the workout with everyone else—front and center. Five minutes later the feeling came back again. This time, I knew I needed to throw in the towel on that class. It just wasn't my day. The old me would never have gone back to that class again. I wouldn't have wanted the girls in the class to think I couldn't handle it. But now I'm confident in my abilities, and I'm not going to let a little feeling of embarrassment prevent me from attending my favorite workout class. So last week, do you know what I did? I went back! Yep. I stuck it out, handled the class, and felt great afterward for having achieved something difficult and overcome my insecurities. I credit this to my confidence.

This applies to the workplace as well, of course. I've walked into the wrong meeting; slipped on a banana peel (no, seriously—I slipped on a banana peel *Mario Kart*–style once); messed up my boss's schedule; made her the wrong kind of iced tea; and a million other embarrassing things. Without confidence, I would have never walked back in those doors. I would never venture outside of my comfort zone. Being confident—not cocky (there's a difference!)—will get you through most situations and enable you to constantly put yourself out there and take initiative.

Okay, so where does confidence come from? It comes from trial and error, experiences, and validation from friends and family. It comes from constantly putting yourself out there, failing, and then watching things eventually work themselves out. My confidence stems from watching so many potential failures turn into success stories over the past few years.

As you grow up, graduate college, and enter the real world, it can be hard to find your identity. Oftentimes you have an idea of who you want to be but you aren't one hundred percent sure—meaning you aren't one hundred percent confident—and that's okay. You're not supposed to be. But over time, you figure out who you are. You know you have your strengths and weaknesses but you are willing to accept them. You know you are going to have embarrassing moments (like that Piloxing class), but you also know that they're ultimately not a big deal. The way we all find confidence is through trial and error, by making mistakes. Confidence comes from experiencing things and just living life. You have no idea how much I wish I could have told my twenty-two-year-old self all of this!

I'm sure that this is a hard concept to take in right now at this point in your life, but think of it as a sign that good things are coming your way. And even though you don't feel too confident right now, just know it's coming.

My friends and I spent so much time in our twenties questioning ourselves in our personal and professional lives. When we look back at the way things have worked out for us, we always say, "If only we knew then, what we know now." Because you know what? We are all just fine. Trust me, in ten years you're going to wish you knew now not to spend so much time and energy worrying about what happens in your day-to-day life.

RULE 2: GET COMFORTABLE BEING UNCOMFORTABLE

Here's another embarrassing story for you (I guess I like these!). When I was sixteen, my parents sent me away for the summer on a teen tour. It's basically forty kids who don't know each other, piled into a big bus for a three-week field trip. Every few days you go to a new city. On our teen tour, we went to Disneyland and Las Vegas, camped in Utah—all over the place. The first week of my trip was a bit of a disaster. It turns out I was the only one without a friend from home with me and didn't have any interest in getting to know anyone else on the tour. I wanted to be with my friends at home. I hated it. At one point I started crying—no, let's be honest, I was bawling—and told my counselor I wanted to go home. When she said no, the relentless side of my personality came out and I threatened to run away if they wouldn't let me leave. I called my parents and told them I was going to run away.

What I didn't tell them was that I was at a campground in the middle of Utah. I wasn't going anywhere, no matter how determined I was. But of course, they told me I had to stick it out and that things would get better. I cried, screamed, and used every curse word I knew at the time. This little episode got me nowhere (do they ever?). I had no choice but to go back to my tent with ten other girls and my counselor. Once I stopped crying, my counselor said to me, "It's the time when you are out of your comfort zone that you grow the most as a person." It was one of those moments when one quick sentence said at the right moment can change your life. Her words have stuck with me ever since, and I use them as a mantra now. By the way, as you might have guessed, the trip ended up being one of the best experiences of my life and I'm so grateful that everyone pretty much ignored me when I threw my tantrum. I made friends that will last a lifetime and had some pretty incredible experiences.

In order to be successful you have to first decide what you want to do, and then constantly put yourself out there, telling people what you want to do. When I was finally ready to move on from the talent agency, I told everyone that I was going to start my own internship company and help college students connect with their dream jobs. When you work at a company that represents the biggest movie stars in the world, leaving it to start your own internship site (or any site at all!) isn't going to be the most popular decision. My coworkers laughed at me and made fun of me behind my back. I was working at such a cool place. They couldn't understand why I'd want to leave and take the risk of failing. I didn't let it stop me. Yes, my feelings were a little hurt and yes, I felt stupid at times, but I kept going and remembered my counselor's words: "It's the time when you are out of your comfort zone that you grow the most as a person." I stuck to that mantra and kept making myself uncomfortable.

After months of telling everyone at my company what I really wanted to do with my life, I got a phone call from a famous movie producer, Marshall Herskovitz, who I'd never met. He asked, "Are you the girl who calls herself the Intern Queen?" I was startled! "Yes . . . how did you know?" Marshall told me that his agent sits down the hall from me and kept overhearing my plans for my business. Marshall ran a site called quarterlife, which catered to college students. He was looking for someone to maintain his following and offer cool internship opportunities while he raised money and developed other projects for the brand. He thought my internship platform idea was perfect. Marshall and I started working together with the understanding that I would stay with him for one year, build my brand, and then we would reevaluate based on the progress of his company. I ended up working with Marshall that year before going off to launch my own business. The lesson here is that you have to tell people what you want to do. Because I told several people that I worked with about my Intern Queen idea, word got around throughout the agency, and my chances of linking up with someone who believed in my idea greatly increased. Although telling everyone at the agency was a very *uncomfortable* experience, the payoff was worth it.

Today, I continue to put myself in uncomfortable situations as frequently as possible. In fact, when I feel myself tensing up or getting scared or insecure about any situation I try to push myself to do it anyway, because I know that forcing yourself outside of your comfort zone forces you to mature and grow.

RULE 3: THINK BIG, FOLLOW THROUGH, EXECUTE

Three years ago, I decided I wanted to have a party in New York for interns in the city. I had three goals for the event: To celebrate the end of the summer internship season, to put together a great panel presentation (the educational value), and to raise brand awareness. My goal was to have at least fifty students show up. I knew nothing about event planning. I'd never thrown a real event before. I was worried that I wouldn't know how to organize all of the information or find enough vendors or that no one would care about my party. For two years, I worked my butt off for this event. I coordinated everything—the DJ, the red carpet, the step and repeat (the banner that celebrities take photos in front of at events), food, drinks, venue, press, promotions, the program of events for the evening—everything. But I knew that in order to really bring my idea to life and to potentially attract sponsors in the future, I was going to have to focus on my execution of the event. If it was a disaster, I would be out a lot of money, time, and energy, and look like an idiot at my first signature company event. My hard work and planning paid off. The first ever Intern Queen party was held at 404, a restaurant and event space in New York City and more than eight hundred young, ambitious interns showed up. It was a giant success and we had great feedback from our attendees.

Two years later I decided I wanted to find a corporate sponsor to help me finance the event and bring it to a whole new level. Again, I had absolutely *no* experience with this concept, and everyone told me it was nearly impossible to snag corporate sponsorship for events. It was hard to meet the right people at big companies and even harder to get them on the phone to pitch the idea and then harder still to actually get them to commit to something. Clearly, I had a lot of work to do. I started doing research, making calls, sending e-mails, and following up with old contacts. I pinpointed a few target brands that I knew I wanted to work with. I stuck to my guns and moved forward. My first step was to put a one-sheet and deck together. A one-sheet is a document that clearly states the who, what, where, when, and why of your idea. It's an opportunity to put all of the pertinent information onto one page so that a potential sponsor can quickly review it and decide if they want to hear more information about your idea. A deck is typically a detailed PowerPoint presentation that you put together about your idea to explain the concept in its entirety to a potential buyer. Once I put my materials together, I built a target list of brands I wanted to sponsor my party. Since the demo for the party was all college students, I put together a list of brands that I thought cared about the college audience and would benefit from being a part of my event. I dug through my e-mails to see which brands I already had contact with and researched the brands I didn't know on LinkedIn and Google. I e-mailed everyone on my target list (twenty companies) and attached my one-sheet and my deck. Out of the twenty companies I reached out to fourteen said no, three never responded, and three said they wanted to set up a call to learn more about the event. Out of those three, one said yes and two said maybe. After many rounds of back-and-forth e-mails and follow up, I landed not one but *three* corporate sponsors for this year's event.

The Intern Queen party stemmed from a simple idea. I was thinking big. I wasn't putting limits on what I could create. I put together a strategy (run the event for two years, make it great, and then go after corporate sponsors). I worked hard on the execution, because a positive result meant I was able to take this project to corporate sponsors. They just needed to put their name on it. The takeaway here is that it's all about the follow-through. The day I said I was going to get a sponsor I immediately got to work, put together a strategy, a timeline, and brainstormed a list of dream sponsors for the event. If I tell someone I am going to do something, I make a point to follow through. I might fail (failure is a part of life and also the path to success), but I make it my business to do what I say I'm going to do.

I was reminded of the importance of the follow-through when I spoke with one of my former Intern Queen campus ambassadors, Melinda Price, who now works for the Autism Community Network (a nonprofit). She said, "The top reasons I've been successful in my postgrad life are determination and willingness to do what it takes to make it work." Melinda doesn't just think big, she follows through and does what she needs to do to get the job done. When she first graduated, she moved to New York City with only an internship and a part-time job. She had no friends and she didn't have a job she was passionate about. Melinda could have easily given up and gone back home but instead she put herself out there, went to networking events, made a group of friends, and eventually got a position at the Autism Community Network. She was thinking big the whole time and knew she had a long way to go, but didn't let that stop her. She didn't let a new situation throw her off. She told everyone of her plan to stay in New York and find a job. She didn't just talk about the idea but she took concrete steps to make it happen. Don't just talk about your big idea—think about the necessary steps you will need to take to get there.

Don't ever let anyone tell you that you are thinking too big. Anything can happen. Anything. We all have our own goals—in our own companies (like mine), at larger corporations, and at boutique firms. Keep using that confidence, getting comfortable being uncomfortable, and thinking big. You can create, develop, and build anything you want.

RULE 4: THINK ABOUT THE CONSEQUENCES

Right after we talk about execution and follow-through is a good time to discuss consequences. One important lesson I've learned over the years, both personally and professionally, is that you have to think about the consequences of your action (or inaction). It's like that moment in the morning when you wake up and think about making your bed. You really don't have any extra energy and have absolutely no desire to make your bed. However, you know what a good feeling it is to slip under the covers at night into that perfectly made bed. It's a great way to end the day and just makes you feel so darn good! Ultimately, you decide to make the bed, because you know your decision will pay off at the end of the day.

You can ignore your e-mails all day but is that going to bite you in the butt tomorrow? Yep. If you don't go in an hour early to start your data entry, are you going to get lost in your day and forget to do it? Probably. Is going out tonight and getting drunk with your friends just going to leave you wishing you were in bed all day tomorrow? Bet on it. Always think about the consequences of your actions. Decide if it's worth it. Hey, sometimes it is, but more often, it isn't.

RULE 5: NEVER SETTLE

I have some friends who are miserable—in their relationships, in their careers, and just in general. They complain about it but they don't fix it. Don't settle. If there is a problem, spend your time figuring out how to fix it. If you get rejected, do your best to pick yourself up and move past it. If you hear yourself constantly repeating the same complaints to friends or family, it might be time to do something about it. Don't settle for an *okay* job—go after your dream job. Don't settle for an okay life—go after that dream life. How can you sit there and constantly say, "What if?" What if you asked for a promotion? What if you apologized? What if you went above and beyond? Keep growing—no matter how old you are, no matter what level you get to. You never know where good work might lead.

RULE 6: LEARN TO LOVE REJECTION, SERIOUSLY

Rejection and I have had our moments over the years, but I'm becoming more and more fond of her. As I continue to grow in my career, first as an intern, then as an employee, and now as an entrepreneur, I've come to realize how large a part rejection plays and will continue to play in my life.

Without realizing it, the people who, through the years, have said no to me have made me prove myself day after day. Without rejection, life would be too easy. We'd have no one to challenge us, no one to motivate us, no one to prove anything to. I first learned about rejection as an intern. I applied to position after position and got one rejection after the next. Each rejection encouraged me to keep going, to push through, and not to give up until someone said *yes*. I decided that if I wanted to do something, I would try my absolute best and not let rejection get in the way. If something didn't happen, after I tried everything in my power, I would simply move on.

When I started my own business, I was already used to rejection, but that didn't make my fear of it any less intense. What if I put my big fabulous idea out into the world and no one cared? What if no one wanted to work with me? What if everyone hung up on me? And to be honest, they kind of did. When I first launched Intern Queen I was rejected left and right. And sure, I took it personally! Remember, my face was on my website—it *was* personal. I remember the stomachaches, the long nights of crying and doubting, the icky feeling in the pit of my gut every time an e-mail started with the word *unfortunately*. But then things began to shift. Every once in a while, I started hearing the word *yes*. And I think through failing time after time, through being rejected again and again, when I finally got that one yes, I looked at it as even more of a victory. When you believe in your idea and what you have to offer, keep going after it; you will find that yes, you will persevere! But remember, rejection is part of the process. Having had enough experience with rejection, I decided I'd be okay if she stayed in my life—I could handle her now.

When I'm on the road speaking at colleges, I tell students and recent grads that I have good news for them. They look at me, waiting for some philosophical advice, and when I say, "You are going to get rejected for the rest of your life," the audience always looks surprised and somewhat skeptical. I go on to explain that we all know we're going to get rejected. It's never smooth sailing for anyone—even the most successful people in the world get rejected on a daily basis.

At your first job, rejection is constant. Your pitches, ideas, concepts, and even your thought processes will get rejected. You try to land your first client—you get rejected. You try to impress your boss—it doesn't work. You try to ask a coworker a question—they ignore you. You finally build up the courage to speak in a staff meeting—rejected again. You get the idea.

Regardless of how you handle rejection, the methods and suggestions below will help. This is a crucial step toward the ultimate goal of bouncing back and moving forward in work and life.

• **VENTING.** You are upset, and that's okay. I find that while venting on the phone to family and friends is a knee-jerk reaction to rejection, it usually isn't the most helpful. When I get rejected, I tend to call my mom, who just tells me to "move on to the next." I always get annoyed, even though she's probably right. "Mom, this was a *big* deal!" I try to make her understand. The whole call is frustrating and I usually end up hanging up quickly. Sometimes calling family and friends can work, but everyone has their own perspectives and experiences that will color their reactions. I've found that it can be helpful to call friends or former colleagues who may be in similar situations and may have experience dealing with what I'm going through. (Be careful about talking to current coworkers though—in case they gossip!) I get rejected everyday—from potential branding deals, speaking engagements, press pitches, and business deals. When this happens I find it helpful to vent to people who also run their own businesses. For me, that's my friend Alyson who runs a PR company or my boyfriend, Michael, who runs an advertising firm. If I have an issue with my staff or team members, I might call my best friend, Meghan, who has a ton of leadership and team-building experience from her role as an executive at Target. And if I just want to whine, complain, and be a big baby, *that's* what my mom is for. She is family and is therefore obligated to put up with me! Look for people who might understand and be able to shed light or offer advice on your situation. Know who to go to in each type of situation. Don't expect too much from people.

• **FUEL YOUR FIRE WITH RAW EMOTION.** One of my former Intern Queen campus ambassadors, Mallory Gold, now works for designer Rachel Roy. Mallory says, "I can't tell you how many times I've heard no but that's what fuels my fire. I want to prove to everyone who has turned me down that it's their loss." Let's face it, rejection can hurt and make us feel downright bad about ourselves. Use that hurt and that anger as motivation to come out bigger and better than the rest. Use it to dominate, to destroy (I mean that in a metaphorical and positive way), and really tackle your next big project, pitch, or assignment. While you are in the heat of the moment, use the power generated from those chaotic emotions to write down new ideas, leads, and other prospects you could go to with your pitch. Let your emotions really add fuel to your fire. You are a rock star. You will persevere. You've got this.

• **MAKE NOTE OF THE FEELINGS.** I was once taught an exercise where every time you feel rejected, you write down what you are physically feeling. For me, it's a nauseating feeling, it's a burning in my chest, it's a pit in my stomach. It's what I describe to friends as the "I feel like an asshole" feeling. Make note of these feelings you get when you are rejected so that you can quickly identify them and take action. Once you understand how your body reacts when you get rejected, you can work to prevent these feelings and quickly take control. Sometimes, all it takes is recognizing the emotion and then you are able to actually do something about it.

• **REJECTION DOESN'T MEAN *NEVER*, IT JUST MEANS *NOT RIGHT NOW*.** In December 2011, I approached Ford to discuss working on a campaign together. I noticed their campaigns for the Ford Focus and Fiesta were both targeted at Millennials. I used LinkedIn (a professional social network you should all be part of!) to target a few marketing executives at Ford to try to pitch my idea. I called one of the executives, Lee Jelenic, whose LinkedIn profile indicated he worked on several Fiesta campaigns and pitched him my idea. Surprisingly, right there on the phone, he told me he liked my idea and gave me his e-mail so I could follow up. And yes, it was that simple! I pitched Ford a unique marketing concept that involved creating Ford-related challenges at different colleges around the country. He responded to my e-mail and told me he was officially interested in working together. Wahoo! I thought a deal was on the horizon. My first big campaign with a major brand. I couldn't believe it. Then, a few weeks later, he called and told me it wasn't going to happen. He ultimately wasn't able to get everyone on board. Ugh, rejection. I felt awful. But instead of giving up, I kept it on my to-do list and checked in with him again a year later (note: be very good at staying in touch with your professional contacts), and asked how everything was going. He called me back right away and said he had just gotten a promotion and might be able to help get my marketing campaign off the ground this time. No way! But then it fell apart again, for whatever reason. A few months later, I reached out to Lee to wish him and his family a very happy holiday season. He responded and said (yep, once again . . .), "Lauren, let's get on a conference call!" I immediately thought, "Here we go again. He's going to get my hopes up and then reject me like the last two times." But hallelujah! This time it was different. He was able to see the campaign through, finally. In February 2013, we launched the Ford College Ambassador Challenge Powered by The Intern Queen Network. My idea was finally brought to life—after years of rejection. Don't underestimate the power of staying in touch and following up with your professional contacts. We'll discuss more of that later in the book. And remember, rejection doesn't mean *never*, it just means *not right now*.

• **DID YOU PUT YOUR CHECK IN THE BOX?** Did you do your best? Did you cover your bases? Really, did you do the *best* you could? At the end of the day, all we can ask ourselves is if we did our best. And if the answer is yes, we put our check in the box, take a deep breath, and call it a night. Remember, as human beings, we aren't mind readers, we won't always know exactly what people want, or how they want the information delivered. We do our best. And that's good enough.

• **UNDERSTAND THAT NO ONE BATS A THOUSAND.** Laura Vanderkam, one of my favorite time-management experts and author of *168 Hours*, reminded me of something when I asked her how she deals with rejection. She says, "You have to understand that no one bats a thousand. You look at the best hitters in baseball and they hit .400. If you accept that rejection is just a numbers game and the more 'at bats' you get, the better the outcome—you can help your brain a bit." Remember, no one is perfect and no one expects you to be. Together, we'll anxiously await that next at bat.

• **THINK ABOUT YOUR SUCCESSES.** Remember that scene in the movie *Clueless* when Cher sends herself flowers to get a boy to notice her? Well, you aren't exactly getting a boy to notice you but you do need to flatter yourself a bit. When you get rejected, take a deep breath, and think about the times in your life when things *have* worked out for you. We all experience our fair share of good news and bad news— acceptance and rejection. When I get rejected, I try to make a list of some of the great things that have happened lately. I focus on those things and remember that sometimes things do work out. This just wasn't meant to be right now. As a motivational speaker, it feels almost ironic to be affected by rejection. I spend so much of my time telling other people not to be affected by rejection, but we all need to stop and remind ourselves of our successes sometimes.

• **ASK FOR CONSTRUCTIVE CRITICISM.** Once you've had a moment to take a deep breath and digest the news, you can ask for constructive criticism. You can say to your boss, to a potential client, to potential new business, "Can I ask what I could do better for next time?" or "Can I ask what compelled you to say no?" You can also say, "Your feedback is much appreciated." Make sure to sound polite and sincere in this approach. You want to make sure your questions don't sound rhetorical or sarcastic. If they respond to you and provide constructive criticism, make note of it for next time and try to apply this knowledge to future projects or pitches. The best thing someone can do once they reject you is to give you constructive feedback to help you in similar situations in the future.

You should also look inward. Ask yourself what *you* think could have been done better. Take some time to reflect and brainstorm and write out what may have potentially gone wrong and what you could do in the future to fix it. In my discussions about rejection with Laura Vanderkam, she shared a great story with me about how she applied for a journalism fellowship, twice. After getting rejected the first time she did a sort of postmortem and evaluated her work. She spoke to people who did get the fellowship about what they put in their applications and studied the biographies of the judges to find subject matter that they could potentially connect with. She also asked herself what she could do differently before applying a second time. She applied again and *got* the fellowship. When rejection rolls around, take it, deal with it, ask for feedback from those who rejected you, and ask yourself what you could do better next time. Apply that information to your situation and go make that deal!

• **KEEP MOVING.** Don't let rejection throw off your day or your week. Rejection can hurt my feelings, make me upset, and make me second-guess myself, but it can't take control of my life. It can't take control of the way I treat others (although it really tries to). It's my job to make sure rejection doesn't get the best of me. One way to move forward is by having multiple projects going on at the same time. I used to get heavily criticized for just having too much going on at any given moment. I never agreed with that criticism. Projects take time and in every industry there is a lot of hurry-up-and-wait. I always have several things brewing at once as you never know when the timing might work out for one project. I mean, you know the old phrase: Don't put all of your eggs in one basket. I find that the more baskets I have, the less likely rejection will ruin my day. If you have several different pitches out and campaigns you are working on, you will always have something else to focus on. When things don't go your way, try to have a to-do list with a ton of other projects you are working on by your side. Then listen to the rejection, take a moment to process it, and move on to the next project. Let your rejection propel you forward onto the next thing. Remember, this will not make or break you. The show must go on.

• **TAKE FIVE.** Sometimes, rejection gets to you and you have to take a moment and step away from your desk. You have to put things in perspective and remember that this rejected deal or pitch or situation isn't your whole life. In fact, work isn't your whole life. And sometimes it takes giving yourself a breather to remember that. When I get rejected from really big projects and just find myself sitting and sulking in my misery, I give myself a break or even a day off—a day to refresh, rejuvenate, a day to come back with the same drive that helped me launch my career. I mentioned earlier that everyone has different ways of dealing with rejection—none are right and none are wrong. Sometimes you need to step away from your work situation for a moment and get control of your feelings before you can move forward, and there is NOTHING wrong with that.

If and when you decide to step away from the office I suggest engaging in an activity that calms you, relaxes you, makes you laugh, or makes you smile. Sometimes having a glass of wine helps but I find that getting wasted and telling the world your problems can lead to even more stress. My go-to relaxation activities are reading books, flipping through a gorgeous fashion magazine and ripping out my favorite pages, completing DIY Projects, playing a round of golf (it's a new thing), going to an upbeat workout class, or even just going for a walk.

Music is helpful, too. Sometimes right after a rejection, I need to have a good cry, throw myself a pity party, and then blast an upbeat song to bring myself out of it. Some of my favorites are "Survivor" by Destiny's Child and "I'm Every Woman" by Whitney Houston. Find your happy song and always keep it on your iPod. Better yet, make a playlist.

REJECTION PLAYLIST

....

My favorite thing to do when I feel rejected is blast music at my house, while on a run, or in my car. Here are hands down some of the best songs to listen to when you feel rejected:

"Survivor"—Destiny's Child

"I'm Every Woman"—Whitney Houston

"Miss Independent"—Kelly Clarkson

"Unwritten"—Natasha Bedingfield

"Tubthumping"—Chumbawamba

"Raise Your Glass"—Pink

"Keep Your Head Up"—Andy Grammer

"Undo It"—Carrie Underwood

"Cruel to Be Kind"—Nick Lowe

"You Oughta Know"—Alanis Morissette

"Stronger (What Doesn't Kill You)"—Kelly Clarkson

"Mean"—Taylor Swift

RULE 7: DON'T TAKE THINGS PERSONALLY

You have to learn to separate your work life from your personal life. At work, rejection isn't personal. Don't take it personally—you will just overthink it. You never know exactly why someone at your company or outside of your company is making a certain decision. Of course, your instinct is to think it's directly related to you or your performance or something you said or did. Most likely, it's not. People make decisions for all kinds of reasons and usually it's chalked up to business as usual and it has nothing to do with you. Next time you are affected by a decision that you don't agree with, take a step back from it and tell yourself not to take it personally. It's not worth your time, anger, or stress.

Learning how to not take things personally is one of the most difficult concepts to wrap your head around as you grow in your environment. It's human nature to want people to love you, respect you, and go out of their way for you. And when they don't, it's hard not to be offended.

If your boss, with whom you have a great relationship, does an annual review with you and doesn't rank you very highly in certain areas (e.g., organization, time management, or client management) they aren't saying that because they don't like you personally. They are saying it as a boss to someone who works for them. They are speaking to your business relationship, not your personal relationship.

It's easy to have these conversations, get very upset, and blame the boss for being "too mean." It's your boss's job to evaluate your work performance, not your personality.

And on the flip side of that, just because someone isn't your best friend in the office, doesn't mean they are going to rank you poorly in an evaluation. I'll talk more about relationships with your superiors in chapter five.

Here's another quick example. As you all know, I'm a business owner. I wasn't a business major in college. I was a communications major. Anything I've learned about business I've really taught myself. When I launched my business in 2009, I had to hire a CPA to keep my business expenses, taxes, payroll, and books in line. I hired a great CPA and for the past few years, I've learned a lot about how to maintain the financial health of a business but I still have tons of questions. My CPA is great in that he does most of the work for me. He sends me the forms, highlights where I need to sign, and keeps me organized. I'm a big believer in learning the process for myself and really trying to understand every form I sign and why I'm signing it. I tend to ask my CPA a ton of questions so that I get a full understanding of how these taxes, laws, and policies work. I want to understand my business from the inside out. Oftentimes, he'll send me an e-mail and I'll write him back with five questions. One time, I got a really bitter response back from him. He thought my questions were offensive and felt like I was questioning his authority or didn't trust his guidance. What he didn't understand was that I was simply trying to learn and understand why we were doing what we were doing. My CPA was taking things personally. I called him right away (always the best way to resolve a conflict) and explained that I thought he was amazing and I was just trying to learn what actually goes on with these policies and processes. He was thankful for the call and I reassured him that I didn't mean it as a personal attack.

Try not to assume the worst right off the bat. Oftentimes, decisions have nothing to do with your sparkling personality; it's just a business decision. And as they say, business is business.

RULE 8: BITCHES AREN'T COOL

Remember in high school when the cool girls were the mean girls? Alert! It's not cool to be the mean girl anymore. On television shows, I always notice the successful woman is either a no-nonsense bitch or a nerd who gets a makeover. Why can't a successful woman be portrayed as friendly or excited or passionate? Why does it always have to go to a negative place? I am a friendly, sometimes silly, vulnerable, excited, passionate person—but no one that knows me would call me weak or unsuccessful.

You don't have to be a bitch to succeed. Don't treat people poorly just because you are having a bad day and don't have an attitude for the sake of having an attitude.

RULE 9: I (TRY TO) STAY BALANCED

One of highlights of this book is that it's not just about the workplace. That first job is about your whole life—your personal life, your romantic life, your financial life, your work life. There are so many things that happen to you when you graduate college and I want to be there to help you navigate. Over the years, I've discovered the importance of balance and doing everything in moderation. During our first years in the working world, of course we're going to stay at work until the wee hours and overdo it. But you have to find that balance so that you can let off steam and truly understand that work is a *part* of life—but work *isn't* life. I'm going to cover staying balanced in chapters eight, nine, and ten where I talk about feeling just too busy, time management techniques, and how to manage and make sure you nurture your personal life. Everyone has the ability to burn out, even those of us who feel we are obsessed with work. Even I burn out sometimes! Balance is important for all of our survival in the workplace, regardless of the type of job you have.

WRAPPING IT UP

After reading through these rules, I hope you can understand why I give so much weight and importance to this chapter. I hope as you read through the rest of the book you will keep these rules in mind. I hope you'll consider them when you think about navigating through your own versions of the real world. Understanding these concepts and tapping into them when appropriate will jolt your career forward. Remember to

- Use your confidence to the best of your ability
- Continue getting comfortable with being uncomfortable
- Think big
- Focus on execution
- Consider the consequences of every decision
- Never settle (for anything)
- Handle rejection like a rock star (well, maybe not exactly like a rock star . . .)
- Don't take things personally
- Watch your attitude
- Seek balance in your day-to-day

And that's about the end of that. I've given you a glimpse into my world, into my mind-set, into my way of doing things and handling myself. Because of these rules and concepts, I've been successful. I continue to abide by these rules today, and they continue to guide me in the right direction.

Next we're going to jump into the actual work you'll be doing at your first, second, and third job. You'll find as we continue to go through the book that you can continue to apply these rules and concepts I've just discussed in almost every section. Feel free to turn back to this chapter as you are going through the book and if you need a pep talk at any time, flip through it again. My heart and soul are in these pillars—these rules to abide by—and I know they will make a huge difference for you. Good luck!

CHAPTER 2

The Actual Work

It's a Thursday. I'm sitting at my chaotic desk trying to get myself organized. My boss isn't in the office so I'm feeling a little more relaxed than usual. As an assistant, you live for the days when your boss is out of the office, in meetings all day, or on an airplane. The phone rings. It's her. "Lauren, I want to have lunch with Robert today. Please schedule." She goes to lunch with Robert, frequently. Robert's favorite restaurant is Katsuya in Hollywood. It is quite a drive from our office in Century City but I knew she would be happy with the choice. I call Katsuya and make a reservation under my boss's name. I pull up her calendar on Outlook (our shared calendar) and enter the following

> Lunch: Ana and Robert
> Location: Katsuya
> Parking: Valet
> Time: 1 p.m.
> Reservation: Under Ana

Ana calls me back. I say, "You're having lunch with Robert at Katsuya at 1 p.m." She says great, hangs up, and I take a deep breath— she's gone for the afternoon! Hooray! I am finally going to have time to get a proper lunch today. What do I want? Thai food? A sandwich?

Matzo ball soup? Hmm . . . I happily start to peruse the menus online. It's about 12:45 and the phone rings again. Uh-oh.

"Lauren, I'm at Katsuya in Brentwood. They don't have a reservation under my name. What is going on?"

"Oh, I didn't realize there were two Katsuyas." (Oh shit!) "I made you a reservation at the Hollywood location," I say slowly.

"Why on earth would I drive from my house in the Palisades to Hollywood and back to Century City? Why would I want to spend the rest of my day in the car?"

Here we go. I never get it right.

"And how am I supposed to know which Katsuya when you don't put the address in the calendar? Am I a mind reader?" She's still going.

"Well, I thought Robert's favorite restaurant was Katsuya in Hollywood and I didn't know there were two Katsuyas. You guys have been before, so I thought you would be happy . . ." I mutter.

"That's Robert Forman! I'm not going with him. I'm going with the writer Rob. Robert Gold."

"Robert Forman *is* a writer." I shoot back to her. I couldn't help myself. I wasn't that stupid.

"Well, I wasn't talking about him. If you were unsure you should have asked. Always ask! Never assume anything."

"I really thought I knew, I'm sorry. Should I change it?" I just want this conversation to end.

"No, Lauren. I will change it. Clearly, you can't do your job, so I will do your job for you. I swear, my seven-year-old niece could do your job better than you."

I try to roll my eyes. I can't. I've been in this situation so many times. And once again, my boss is right, I should have asked questions and been more detail oriented. I shouldn't have made assumptions on who she was meeting and I should have predicted a potential mistake.

You work so hard to get the job. You sweat and stress yourself out beyond belief to get through the application and interview process. And then the offer comes. You finally land that dream job or the job that might be able to get you to your dream job, and you are in a state of euphoria. How can life get any better? You plan, prepare, and psych yourself up for that big first day. Your clothing is picked out, your nails are freshly manicured, and you even get a blow out! You play the image of the ideal first day of work over and over in your head. And then it finally arrives. You have the best first day on the job—ever! And then what? What happens two weeks later when the job isn't so new anymore?

You sold yourself to get the job. Now it's time to prove what you sold. You stressed yourself out about the job. You thought about it day and night. But now it's actually here and you have to continue to put just as much energy into your work as you did in landing the job.

You might think that you are the best at your job. You come in every day on time. You even answer e-mails on the weekend. You know you have a great work ethic. But how is your actual work? Do things always get scheduled? Do e-mails always get handled in an orderly fashion? Do you meet deadlines? Do you put together the best papers and research projects? Do you manage your clients in the best way possible?

When your work is better, you are better. I don't think I really understood that at twenty-two. I thought that as long as I showed up and did as I was told, I was going to impress my boss. I didn't understand that just because I was friendly and came to work on time didn't mean I was good at my job. My actual work was awful! I was a natural multitasker. I could eat a hamburger, drive, and talk on the phone at the same time, so I figured this would naturally translate to my job. Turns out, I was wrong. Amazingly, my dangerous vehicular habits did not set me up for success in the real world. I had a lot to learn.

I still have nightmares about all the things that I messed up day after day. Listen: You will make a lot of mistakes. But in making those mistakes, you will finally learn the right way to get things done—the effective way to do your job. Today, I hold myself and my work to a certain standard. When I got hired, I wish someone explained what that standard was. Here is your chance to understand how to do great work at your first, second, or third job.

MAP IT OUT

Before we dive into specific tasks, I want to explain the importance of not just following the systems already in place, but also implementing new systems within your role. Though you don't often think about it, systems are a big part of everyone's life. When I go downstairs in my apartment building to check the mail, I have a system. I scan through the envelopes while standing at the mailbox; I recycle anything that looks like junk, coupons, or credit card sign-ups and take the real mail upstairs. Before I take more than three steps into my apartment, I have a small tray where I place all of my bills and anything that needs to be handled promptly. I stick any thank-you notes or wedding invitations (I'm in that phase of life where you get a ton of wedding invites) on my refrigerator, and put the bank statements or information I might need to file into my desk drawer. Voilà! My mail has been handled according to my system.

Everything you are responsible for at work should have a system, and you should make these systems your own. Don't just keep doing something a particular way because the person who had your job before did it that way. You'll be much more effective if you organize things in a way that's easiest for you. And you can keep perfecting your system through trial and error. Not only will this get things done faster and more accurately, but if your boss sees you taking initiative in this way you'll look really good! Start by writing down all of the tasks you are responsible for and what your method is for processing those tasks when they come across your desk. For example, one of my duties at the agency was to send scripts to clients (movie stars) when my boss requested them. My process map for that task looked like this:

- My boss e-mails me a script name.
- I look it up either by title of project or writers/producers attached.
- I double check that this is the correct script.
- Once confirmed, I follow the formatting rules and send a letter to the client encouraging him/her to take a look at the script.
- I bring the letter into my boss's office so that she can sign it and approve it.
- I stick the script and letter in a manila envelope and stick it in the out-box on my desk.
- I call the client a few hours later to confirm that he/she got the script.

It's a long process, but one I knew well and followed religiously. Another shorter example is the phone system. The phone rings. Your boss isn't available? What is the protocol? Are you supposed to say they are busy? In a meeting? Have stepped away from their desk? And what information are you supposed to take down from the caller? First and last name, phone number, company name. What is the call about? And where do you put the message? Do you have a phone sheet document that you share with your boss? Do you leave a note on their desk? Are you supposed to send them a text message? Asking these questions and laying out the answers in an orderly fashion is how office systems are created.

What are your processes going to be for the different things that get thrown your way? I encourage you to make a list of the top five to ten most common tasks you are asked to do in the office. Do they include scheduling meetings? Brainstorming? Researching? Putting together lists? Handling social media? Creating proposals? What are the universal systems already in place to handle these tasks? If the company already has clear systems in place, you are going to want to follow them. Take the time to really understand them, ask questions if need be, and make sure you really take these systems seriously. These systems will help you understand your work and the manner in which it should be executed. Typing up this information will keep you organized and if you ever need to call in sick or train someone to take over your position, you'll already have the processes typed out and will save a ton of time.

If you feel you understand what the company wants the final product to be and that isn't coming across in the system—change it up. Ask your boss if you can experiment with a different way of getting something done. Efficiency only helps the entire team. If there is a task you are often asked to do and there is no system for it—create one. You and your colleagues or team members should be on the same page about how your company gets things done.

If you have questions about how any process should work, speak to your boss or the person who trained you. Make a list of your questions ahead of time and then group them together if possible to take the least amount of your boss's time.

KNOW THE PLAYERS

Something you should do right away when you start a new job (especially if you're assisting someone specific) is to learn who the major players are—that is, who does your boss interact with on a daily and weekly basis? Learn a few details about those people like which restaurants they prefer, which time zone they live in, and their relationship to your boss. This will be invaluable to making the calls go smoothly.

SCHEDULE THE PERFECT PHONE CALL OR MEETING

These entry-level jobs contain their fair share of scheduling, for both yourself and your boss. When scheduling calls or meetings, you must be detail oriented. Remember my example at the beginning of the chapter when I sent my boss to the wrong restaurant? You can learn from my mistakes!

Whenever you schedule a meeting between two people (or more), you need to get the following information:

- First name and last name of all parties attending
- Time and time zone: Time zone is very important. You have to ask people what time zone they are in. And people travel so much these days that even if the person's e-mail signature says New York, they might be traveling to Los Angeles that week.
- Location of the meeting: If it's at an office building you need the floor and suite number. Always include the zip code to make it easier for people to look it up on Google Maps or on a GPS.
- Location phone number: Anticipate the problems, just in case your boss needs to call ahead for some reason.
- Parking information: Call the store or restaurant or office building ahead of time and ask for their parking details. Also find out if validation is required so your boss knows if they need to bring their parking ticket inside.
- Contact phone numbers: You should have the cell phone numbers for everyone attending the meeting. You could include their office phone number and assistant's information as well.

Whenever you schedule a phone call or conference call between two or more parties, you need to get the following:

First name and last name of the parties attending
Time and time zone: Just like I said above, this is super important.
Location of the call: For example, is one person calling the other direct? Are they all calling in to a conference line? If they are, what is the number and what is the dial-in code?
Contact phone numbers and e-mails: You need this just in case

someone is running late or one party wants to e-mail another during a call.

Remember, all of this information should be entered into the shared calendar at work. Be sure to indicate if it's a call or meeting when you enter the information. For example, if I was putting a call in my calendar, it would look like this

MONDAY, APRIL 9 @ 12 P.M. PST
CALL: LAUREN BERGER/ALDO SHOES MARKETING TEAM
ATTENDEES: LAUREN BERGER, MYRA GOLDBERG (ALDO), SHERRY DAWSON (ALDO)
CONFERENCE LINE: 712-775-7300
DIAL-IN CODE: 437171
CONTACT INFO: LAUREN@INTERNQUEEN.COM, MYRA@ALDO.COM, SHERRY@ALDO.COM
SHERRY AND MYRA PHONE: 212-555-7899

Here's another example for a meeting that is entered into your calendar:

MONDAY, APRIL 9 @ 12 P.M. PST
MEETING: LAUREN BERGER/MICHAEL KENNY (AARROW ADVERTISING)
LOCATION: COFFEE BEAN TOLUCA LAKE
1231 RIVERSIDE DRIVE
TOLUCA LAKE, CA 91505
818-555-1212
PARKING: FORMAN AND RIVERSIDE PARKING LOT
CONTACT INFO: MICHAEL KENNY (MKENNY@AARROWADS .COM/619-555-5555)

IF YOU ARE ASKED TO RUN A CALL

Create a power agenda. Whenever your boss asks you to lead a meeting or a call, make sure to put together an agenda. This is a quick way to look like you know what you are talking about and to take control of the conversation. When you start the call, introduce yourself and go over the list of items you'll be covering. This will show your boss how competent you are and give you a chance to really prove yourself to both your boss and to the client. Don't get nervous, and if you do, recover quickly. Take a deep breath before you start the call and let that nervous energy lead you in the right direction.

PROFESSIONAL PHONE ETIQUETTE

We already talked about how to schedule conference calls. Now, we must discuss phone etiquette. On one of my first days at my first job, I was manning the phones. It was pretty easy; I answered the phone, "Ana Jones's office." The other person asked for Ana. I responded with, "May I ask who's calling?" Once I got the name, I asked them to hold please. I would ask Ana if she wanted to take the call. If she said yes, I put it through. If she said no, I said, "I don't have her. Can we return?" I asked for their number if we didn't have it.

Seems easy, right? So on one of my first days I was practicing this phone back and forth. I got a call from someone, but I couldn't understand his name. I wasn't too familiar with Ana's clients, friends, and coworkers yet. I said my typical, "May I ask who's calling?" He said, "It's Reeve Buhemi." I said, "I'm sorry, who?" "Reeve Buhemi." I wasn't sure exactly what he said. He spoke fast. I yelled at Ana (this is how we operated). I said to Ana, "I have Reeve Buhemi on line one." "Who?" she yelled back. "Reeve Buhemi." "Lauren, I don't know who that is." "I mean, I think that's what he said."

At this point, at least seven assistants have started listening to our back and forth. Here I was, supplying the office entertainment as usual. Ana grunted. She picked up the phone in a hurry. "Hi, this is Ana." "Hey Ana!" "Steve?" "Yep," he said. "Oh my god, my assistant is new and she told me someone named Reeve Buhemi was calling." Ha! She laughed, making fun of me. He laughed. It was *Steve Buscemi*, the movie star.

And once again, I take the cake on embarrassing moments at the office. Before you start on the phones I suggest getting acquainted with your boss's phone sheet and client roster, and ask whoever is training you for a list of the people who call the most frequently. Practice reading through their names out loud; you don't want to mess this up like I did.

QUICK PHONE TIPS

• **RELAX.** Stay cool, calm, and collected on the phone. People can sense your insecurity. Even when it's your first month or two on a new desk or at a new job, speak slowly, clearly, and if you can't understand someone's name, ask them politely to repeat it. Trust me, if they are calling, they want to make sure they get a returned phone call and if you mess up the name—that's not going to happen.

• **BE PERSONABLE.** Make the person on the other line feel comfortable. Build relationships with the people calling your office by actually acknowledging them, sounding excited to hear them, repeating their name. By the time I got comfortable at my boss's desk, I would answer the phone and say, "Hello so and so. Great to hear from you! How are you? How was your trip?" I was aware of the person and even one step beyond that, I was aware of what they were up to. People will appreciate the personal attention and they will remember you and request to speak with you because of it.

• **MIND THE 'TUDE.** Never lose your temper, be rude, or snippy with people on the phone—you never know who is on the other end of the line. You have to treat everyone with the same respect and have the "everyone knows everyone" mentality. Also, you might meet these people in person one day. If you are nasty to them on the phone, that will be an awkward interaction. Not to mention that if your boss hears that you were rude, she's not going to be thrilled. Remember, you are a representative of their brand, their office, and of your company. If you are out of line, it can reflect poorly on your boss and even your company. Sometimes you will be the first real human from the company that the person on the other line connects with. Be careful.

• **TAKE NOTES AND FOLLOW UP.** When you are in charge of answering the phones, you should always have a piece of paper and pen handy as you never know who is going to call or what sort of message or assignment they might leave for you. Make sure to take very clear notes, follow the system your boss has in place for transferring messages, and make sure the message gets to where it needs to go. If the person on the phone made a request, make sure to follow through with it. Don't let messages get crumpled up on your desk somewhere. Make sure the call sheet doesn't go missing. Take notes and then follow up with whatever phone promises you make.

E-MAIL ETIQUETTE

In 2004, I got an internship with PR guru Warren Cowan (of Rogers and Cowan fame). Warren was quite the mentor. Although I met him toward the end of his life and his hugely successful career, I learned a ton. All his notes to people were handwritten, and he dictated his e-mails. Old school, right? By 2004, almost everyone was using e-mail as the go-to form of communication, but not Warren. He knew he had to e-mail but really wasn't a fan of it. I would sit in the corner of his office and type his e-mails for him. He would write letters. He loved this personal touch, and the people who worked with him, the legends—Elton John, Paul Newman, and Frank Sinatra—appreciated him for his traditional, classic style. I learned from Warren that there is a way to marry the two styles and include a personal touch. Although most of my professional correspondence happens via e-mail, I'm always writing thank-you notes and birthday cards to people. Go out of your way to send someone a handwritten note every once in a while. Trust me, it goes a long way.

In our world today, inboxes are like a popularity contest. Who gets the most e-mails? Who has the most clutter to dig themselves out of? You'll find yourself falling into the trap of comparing your inboxes with your colleagues. "I have forty-three e-mails in my inbox just in the last hour!" "Yeah? I have fifty-two. Crazy, right?" The busiest person, the person with the most e-mails, always wins! First of all, *this is not a contest you actually want to win*. Second, whether you like it or not, e-mail etiquette is crucial for survival in today's workplace. Every time you communicate with a professional contact it should be nothing but professional. I hired an assistant a few months back and texted her asking if she completed a task. Her response was, "Dude, I did it!" I was shocked. Was this person confused? Did she think we were friends? Why did she feel comfortable enough to call me *dude*? Needless to say, she didn't stay with me very long.

In Ivanka Trump's book, *The Trump Card: Playing to Win in Work and Life*, she talks about the importance of professionalism when e-mailing, as you never know where that e-mail will go. Ivanka warns young people to stay away from the short, one-word e-mails as you never know who is reading them. You always want to cover your tracks. You also want to make sure that e-mails don't come across as ungrateful, annoyed, or as being "short." E-mails are like text messages: You can't always understand the tone. Here are a few things to remember:

LEARN TO LOVE THE DRAFT E-MAILS

Once you identify the tasks you will do repeatedly at your new job, start to create e-mail drafts. You can have drafts for everything—meeting e-mails, where-to-park memos, confirmation e-mails, and more. Having these on hand will help you do your job efficiently, and can act as a secondary to-do list as well if you refer to your draft inbox regularly.

E-MAIL STRUCTURE

• **WATCH ATTACHMENTS.** It may seem obvious, but it happens all the time. If you are sending an e-mail with an attachment, first make sure the file is attached. The file should also have an appropriate, relevant, and professional name. Also, make sure that if you are attaching multiple files they are in some sort of order and that order is referenced in the body of the e-mail.

• **PERSONALIZE IT.** Always start by acknowledging the person. I usually start with, "Hope you are well." If you know something personal about him or her, feel free to throw it in. "I remember you mentioned being in Hawaii last week with your family. I'm so jealous and can't wait to hear about it!" Maybe it sounds fake to you, but you're making an honest effort to better connect with the person and that personal touch is so often appreciated by the individual on the other end.

• **BE MINDFUL OF THE LENGTH.** Try to keep your e-mail short and concise but not too casual. No one wants to read an e-mail that goes on for days. If I get an e-mail in my inbox that's more than two paragraphs, I'm likely to file it away and look at it later. You want to make sure people are able to quickly read and decipher what you are sending them. On the other hand, stay away from one-word e-mails. You need to make sure you address every question in order to avoid any back and forth (more e-mails!).

• **BE CONSIDERATE OF THEIR TIME.** You'll hear this more than once from me, but executives are extremely sensitive about their time. They don't want it to be wasted. At the end of a professional e-mail thank the person for her time and tell her you look forward to connecting in the future.

• **WATCH THE RECIPIENT LIST.** Pay attention to the order of the recipients on an e-mail chain. For example, if I'm e-mailing my boss, her colleagues, and their assistants, I'm going to start with my boss's name and then list the recipients in order of importance or seniority at the company. I suggest asking your boss if your e-mail CCs should be in a specific order. Usually the other assistants or support staff will just be CCs on the e-mail.

• **REVIEW YOUR CCS.** On your e-mails, you have a CC bar and a BCC bar. Make sure that the people who are supposed to be copied on the e-mail, are on the e-mail. If you share clients with a team of coworkers at your job, you want to check and see if they should be copied on your client-related e-mails. You also want to make sure you don't accidentally put the wrong people on e-mails. People get very upset when they aren't included (CC'd) on e-mails they are supposed to be included on. It's a quick way in the professional world to make someone feel unimportant and out of the loop.

• **WATCH OUT FOR FORWARD AND REPLY ALL.** Be aware of the REPLY ALL button. This button can get you in a LOT of trouble. Don't accidentally send a message to someone you didn't mean to send it to. Double check who the message is going to before you hit send. For example, my friend Sarah hates going to parties that feel like frat parties. She hates beer, beer pong, flip cup, and everything that comes along with a "red-cup house party." Last week, another friend e-mailed Sarah and me and said, "Hey Gals, you must come to my friend's party.

We will have tons of beer, kegs, and good ole fashioned house party fun." She described everything that Sarah despises. I was hysterically laughing. I forwarded the e-mail back to Sarah and said sarcastically, "OMG, your favorite things all in one place!" EXCEPT I accidentally hit the REPLY ALL button and the girl who sent us the invitation got the e-mail. She knew I was being sarcastic. She wasn't too upset (or at least she didn't tell me she was), but she definitely hasn't invited us to a party in a while. The same thing goes for the FORWARD button. Make sure you are watching the FORWARD button and removing people that shouldn't be copied on your e-mails.

• **DOUBLE-CHECK SENDER.** Double-check the person you are sending the e-mail to. If I want an e-mail to go to Samantha Nifakos at CNN, I don't want to accidentally send it to Samantha Nifakos (someone with the same name) at the mayor's office. If they are both in my Outlook address book that makes it tricky. I always have to make sure to double-check. It's an easy mistake to make and could be very embarrassing.

• **BEWARE OF THE PAPER TRAIL.** Watch what you put in an e-mail. Once it's in an e-mail, there is a paper trail and it can get back to you. If you don't want a conversation to bite you in the behind, do it over the phone, not over e-mail. Remember, you never know who will see this e-mail. Once you hit SEND—it's out of your control forever. Don't write anything you wouldn't want someone else to see.

• **CHECK THE BCC.** If someone BCCs you on an e-mail, it typically means the point of the e-mail is to make you aware of the information and keep you in the loop, but it doesn't mean that you should directly respond. In fact, usually if you are BCC'd it means the person sending the e-mail doesn't want you to respond. Usually, they don't even want the person the e-mail was sent to realizing that you were on the e-mail. If you aren't sure if the e-mail requires a response, ask your supervisor.

• **CLOSE THE E-MAIL APPROPRIATELY.** I always sign my professional e-mails "Best," and then include my e-mail signature. Your e-mail signature should already be set up, but if it's not, you should at least have the following information:

> **Lauren Berger (First and Last Name)**
> **Founder and CEO (Position/Title)**
> **"The Intern Queen" (Company Name)**
> **www.internqueen.com (Company Website)**
> **Office: 818-433-7240 I Direct: 727-555-5555**
> **E-mail: lauren@internqueen.com**
> **Twitter: @internqueen I Facebook: InternQueen**
> **Book: *All Work, No Pay***

Please note: I include my business phone and cell phone. You can include what you find appropriate. Some companies don't want your cell on your e-mail signature. Other companies will want you to include an extension number.

FIO: FIGURE IT OUT

Are you ready for the cold harsh reality about the real world? It's simple. You can't say things like, "I can't," "I don't know," or "I haven't figured it out." Because if you don't figure out solutions—if you don't pride yourself on finding solutions to problems—your boss will be disappointed with your lack of initiative. You are an employee now and no matter what your job description is, I promise that being resourceful is buried in there somewhere. If there is a problem, if something is broken, if a situation isn't working correctly—they expect you to figure it out.

If I ask an employee to work on a research project and they call me and say, "I've got nothing," I find that extremely frustrating. They are basically saying, "I can't do it. You do it." And it's now up to me to do their work. When you can't find the answers you are looking for, think outside the box and find a way to get it done. Be strategic. Where else can you look? Who can you speak to? Who could you get in touch with that might know the answer to that question? Don't give up. Also, don't be too proud to ask questions. When you don't know how to do something, don't be afraid of asking coworkers for help. They'd rather you ask questions than take a guess and mess up.

Here's a quick example from my first job. Once, my boss called me in the middle of the night. She was in Italy traveling with her family. She told me that she bought a designer soap and left it at a restaurant she went to that evening. She didn't know the name of the restaurant or where it was located. She just told me to find the soap and have it sent to her hotel and hung up the phone. My job was to locate a random bar of soap at a random restaurant somewhere in Italy at midnight. Seriously? I had no idea where she went to dinner but I knew I couldn't just call my boss back and say, "I don't know where the soap is." That was not an option. I did know the name of the hotel where my boss was staying because I had made her travel itinerary. I called the hotel and asked to speak with the concierge (trying not to think too much about my phone bill). I knew my boss well enough to know that she would have asked the concierge for a dinner recommendation. Sure enough, he knew the exact restaurant and gave me the number. I phoned the restaurant and of course—no one spoke English. I then called the hotel back, explained the situation, and asked if the concierge could call the restaurant and have someone pick up the soap. I told him we'd cover the expense of that. It worked! We found the soap! I thought outside the box and I got my job done by thinking creatively. The answer wasn't right in front of me but I didn't give up. Don't give up. Find a solution and FIO—figure it out.

UTILIZING YOUR NETWORK FOR RESEARCH

Now we get to the power of your personal and professional networks. As you grow in your career, your network will become more and more powerful. With tools like LinkedIn and Facebook, your network will end up helping you in many situations when you need information and when you need intros. For example, I had a former Intern Queen campus ambassador e-mail me and ask if I knew anyone who worked in South Korea. She told me she was moving there after college and wanted to pursue a career in the business world. My initial reaction was, "I don't know anyone in South Korea." I decided that just to be sure, I would check my social networks. I looked at my LinkedIn page and typed *South Korea* into the search bar. Sure enough, someone I'd met at a human resources conference in 2009, who I was connected with on LinkedIn, had relocated to South Korea about a year ago. He was working for Hyundai in human resources. I immediately reached out via LinkedIn and introduced him to my former campus ambassador. Never underestimate the power of your personal and professional networks.

HOW TO DO PERFECT RESEARCH

My friend Shannon was recently sent by her company to Montreal for the Montreal Comedy Festival—a yearly showcase of the best comedians in the world. Shannon's job is to go to the festival, attend as many comedy shows as possible, and determine which comics her company should consider doing business with. After the festival, she is responsible for putting together an entire research project with information on the comedians that she feels were the standouts from the festival. This project gets distributed to all of the major executives within the company. To ensure her project was up to par and beyond impressive Shannon did the following:

- While at the festival, she took clear and thorough notes on each comedian and show she attended.
- She kept copies of each show's program so that she would have all of the necessary information on each comic. For her project, this was the research material.
- She kept all of the business cards she collected from comedians and other executives at the festival in a plastic bag so they wouldn't get ruined or disappear. She did the same thing with her expenses—which I'll discuss in a bit.
- To make sure she kept her notes fresh in her mind, she organized them and highlighted the important information she wanted to include in her presentation while she was flying home.
- As soon as she returned to work, she immediately made the project a priority. She knew the importance of turning in the material in a timely manner while the festival was still relevant and being buzzed about. Do the work while it's fresh in your mind. The longer you wait, the more trouble you will have turning your notes into a report.
- Shannon entered her notes and organized them into a Power-Point presentation to go above and beyond what her superiors were expecting.
- To continue to go above and beyond, Shannon didn't just include her notes, she also took the time to look up each comedian she was entering information about and included a photo of them and links to their YouTube channels so that the executives could easily visualize and access the information she was presenting.

Needless to say, her boss was impressed. Points for Shannon!

THINK AHEAD. PREDICT THE NEXT PART OF THE RESEARCH

Using my Shannon example, you can see that she anticipated what her boss wanted and predicted the next step. Once her boss read about the comedians Shannon enjoyed, she probably would have asked Shannon for links to watch their performances. Shannon was one step ahead and already included that information. Shannon anticipated her boss's needs.

Let's look at an example of something you could do in this situation. Let's say you work at a public relations company and your boss just signed a new young female celebrity to her roster. She sends you to Barnes & Noble to look at the female celebrities featured in teen magazines to understand where the company should try to place their new client. You bring your notepad or computer and start taking notes. Here is where thinking ahead, being detail oriented, and predicting the next step come into play. Of course, you'll write down the name of the magazine and the celebrities featured. But take this a step further. Think about why she sent you there in the first place and what her follow-up questions are likely to be. Then you can anticipate them. Your boss is probably going to want to know which section of the magazine the celebrity is featured in and which editor is responsible for that section. Go the extra mile and write it down. You could even take it a step further by taking pictures of the sections on your phone to include in your report.

UNDERSTAND THE PRIORITY LEVEL OF YOUR RESEARCH TASK

Make sure to determine how much time your boss wants you to spend on each research project. You don't want to get stuck on one research project, spend all day hunting information down, and then have your boss look at you like you are crazy and say, "I didn't want you spending all day on that! You should have spent five minutes and moved on. It wasn't priority." You aren't a mind reader. You have to ask questions in order to get inside your boss's mind. The easiest way is just by asking, "How long do you want me to spend on this?" The worst thing is to spend five hours on a project that your boss only wants you to spend five minutes on. Not all research projects are top priority. Ask, ask, ask! Once you get in the habit of asking questions, you'll soon be able to anticipate your boss's needs and you'll know what the priorities are.

HOW TO KEEP DATABASES LOOKING PERFECT

Many companies have ongoing lists that different entry-level employees are responsible for keeping up to date. They use these lists to track everything from the newest restaurants in town to who the competition might be representing. These projects can often seem overwhelming, as sometimes these lists haven't been properly maintained in the past. Here are my tips for managing these lists and overwhelming projects:

• **UNDERSTAND THE COMPANY SYSTEM AND PROCESSES AND FORMATTING.** A friend of mine just started a job in the hospitality industry. She spent seven hours one day entering data (sounds fun, right?) and after every cell she entered, she included a period. The next day, one of her coworkers told her the company really hates when periods are entered into the cells on Excel sheets. She warned that they would probably make her do it over. She was right. The next day her boss called her in and told her the periods would need to be taken out of each column ASAP. After another seven hours of correcting her mistake, she learned that you should always ask about company formatting policies ahead of time. Ick.

• **SET ASIDE A CHUNK OF TIME TO HANDLE THESE LISTS AND TO COME UP WITH A STRATEGY.** Manage your supervisor's expectations and let them know when you plan on being finished. Make sure there is no deadline date that you should be aware of before you have this conversation. Decide how much time you'll spend on the project every day. Set a goal to get through a certain amount every day or every morning.

• **NEVER BUILD UPON POOR WORK.** Even if you have to start from scratch and make more work for yourself, it's better to start these lists over, reformat them, and do them the correct way. Say you work at an interior design firm and your boss asks you to manage the current client list. You get the list and it's a disaster with poor formatting, no flow, and several different fonts. The entire list is almost impossible to read. You decide that you are going to need to scrap the list and build it from scratch to make it easier to read and a more useful tool in the office. You are not only going above and beyond the expectations but you are adding major value to the company by taking the time to do this.

• **REMEMBER, ONCE A PROJECT HAS BEEN PASSED ON TO YOU, YOU ARE RESPONSIBLE FOR MAINTAINING IT.** Even though someone else started it, your name is on it. And trust me, you will be blamed if it's not kept up to par. When a partner at the company asks to see the list and it doesn't look good, they are going to blame you—not the person who was responsible for it before you. Once you are handed a project, take full ownership and do whatever you need to do to make it look amazing.

KEEP EXPENSES LOOKING PERFECT

Another popular entry-level task is tracking and submitting your boss's expenses. At most companies, your boss has a company credit card and spends money on lunches, dinners, drinks, travel, and parking. Of course, the assistant is usually responsible for taking these receipts, organizing them, scanning them, and plugging each expense into an Excel document or online program so the accounting department can process the charges and reimburse your boss. Sometimes expenses can total thousands and thousands of dollars so this task is a priority for many executives. If one receipt gets lost they could have to pay lots of money out of pocket to cover something that the company should have been covering. Because the amount of money gets so large, most businesses have strict rules about how expenses must be submitted to the accounting department, the information required, and the amount of time that can have elapsed between a business meeting and when the expenses from that meeting are submitted.

Here are a few hints on how to handle expenses:

- Put a folder on your desk and label it Expenses so that your boss always puts them in the right place.
- Ask what the process for expenses is and keep a checklist on a memo or buck slip. Make sure you complete everything on the checklist every time you do expenses.
- Schedule thirty minutes twice a week on your calendar to go through the expenses and organize them.
- Instead of scanning them, take quick photos of them on your phone, that way you can easily transfer all of them to your computer.
- Deal with them when they are in front of you. If you can't submit all of them until you have more information, immediately write on the back who your boss was with and the purpose of the expense. Start tracking them on an Excel sheet so the information is there when you need it. It's crucial to make sure the expenses get done in a timely manner.
- Let your boss know about any receipts you might be missing. Do this quickly. If you wait too long, the company might give your

boss a hard time about them. Ask your boss if there are any credit card charges that you should look into.

- If you are able to get reimbursed for office expenses, have a separate part of your wallet where you always put your receipts. Then, make sure you take these out and properly submit them. If you don't learn your lesson now, you certainly will the first time you have to pay out of pocket to cover an expense or late fee!

And that wraps up this chapter on the nuts and bolts of everyday office work. I hope after reading this chapter you feel more knowledgeable and confident about what is required and expected of you in terms of day-to-day tasks in an entry-level job. I'm glad we had the opportunity to review the importance of

- Systems—learning to map out your processes
- Scheduling phone calls and meetings
- Phone and e-mail etiquette
- How to FIO—figure it out
- How to perfect your research
- Perfect your databases
- Perfect your expense reports

I know that all of you will have other tasks come across your desks that consume the majority of your days, but this will start you off right, as most office jobs will require these general tasks.

I probably would have been twenty times better at my job had I read back then what I just wrote for all of you. It seemed like I screwed up every e-mail, every calendar invite, and every phone call—and made every embarrassing mistake possible. Today, I'm still in touch with my first boss and we laugh about my mistakes that very first year. I'm glad we can look back and laugh at it now, because at the time— she definitely did NOT think it was funny!

CHAPTER 3

Organize, Prioritize, Maximize, and Other *-ize* Words

Flashback time. Remember when I told you about my chaotic, crazy desk at the talent agency? Today, that messy desk is no more. I've finally gotten to a place where it looks organized and put together. Yes, I have my fair share of girly Intern Queen flair—but everything is presented in a very organized fashion. My sparkle notebooks are all color coded depending on what project I'm using them for; the pens are in the pen mug; my folders are labeled To Pursue, To Handle, and To File. My desk looks awesome if I do say so myself. And I was formerly known as the messiest girl in the world (seriously). But if I can change, you can change. Organization is power. When you are organized, you can easily access information—and that is powerful. Organization is only the beginning. In this chapter we're going to explore three of my favorite words: Organize, prioritize, and maximize. I have tips—and these tips are going to help you get your work life together. Get excited!

ORGAN-IZE
Make Sure Nothing Slips Through the Cracks
I'm going to put on my employer hat and be tough on all of you for

a moment. You are not good at your job until nothing—I repeat—*nothing* falls through the cracks. There is no worse mistake than when an important task is delegated and then is forgotten about or pushed too far down on the list of priorities. Even if it's one e-mail that you miss or one person you forget to get back to, letting things slip through the cracks is a very visible sign of disorganization. Let me give you an example of something that could happen to you in the office. Sandra works at a very well-established marketing firm in San Francisco. She has only been working at the company for about six months but her boss is already letting her run point on a big client. The campaign is in the beginning stages and every detail matters. It's a new client and it's big business—she doesn't want to mess up. She coordinates an initial call with the client via e-mail. She tells the client to plan on a call for 4:30 P.M. to discuss the strategy for the campaign. Sandra sends out an e-mail to the entire team (and the client) confirming the time of the meeting, the time zone, the call-in number, and the full names of the people attending the call. Sandra feels on top of her game and excited to really use this opportunity to prove herself to her boss. She's going about her day and responding to e-mails when she looks at the clock—it's 4:45 P.M.—SHIT! She is fifteen minutes late for the phone call. She doesn't have an excuse—she just forgot. Her entire team and the client are waiting on the call. Before she can dial-in she gets an e-mail from the client, who says, "I've been waiting on the conference line with YOUR team for fifteen minutes. I'm hanging up now. This was a waste of time. Let's reschedule." And if that wasn't bad enough, she copied Sandra's boss on the e-mail. Almost immediately, Sandra's boss calls her into the office. Sandra gets taken off the account, just like that. Her boss explains to her that the client pays the company millions of dollars each year; if the client gets upset and leaves, she might get fired. Sandra is usually very good at her job, but that's not enough. If she were as organized as she should be, she would have put that phone call in her calendar. And because that one conference call fell through the cracks, she doesn't get her chance to prove herself to her boss. In fact, it's probably going to take her a while to be in a situation where she can prove herself to her boss in the future. Be careful about letting things slip. As you saw in this example, sometimes when you let things fall through the cracks, it doesn't just affect you, it affects your boss, and it can also affect superiors who you don't even see on a daily basis. You never know the end result of a mistake—so try your hardest to prevent them at all costs.

Today, I can't stand when things slip through the cracks. Turns out I'm just like my former boss. If a member of my team misses an e-mail, doesn't get back to someone in a timely manner, or forgets to do something, it drives me crazy. It makes me feel like they aren't in charge of their work; their work is in charge of them. And it's such an easy thing to fix. That's why I can't stress these calendars and to-do lists enough. It's so important to track everything so that nothing falls through the cracks. When this happens, not only do you look bad, but the company looks bad.

The Perfect Work Space

When I started my first job I moved right into a messy desk. The girl who held the position before me didn't organize anything so I was left with the remains. I had no time to organize it and kept telling myself I would get to it *eventually*. Don't fall into this trap! I encourage you to go in over the weekend (I know, it sounds painful) and put on some music and get it done. Take a few hours out of your day (Saturday, and Sunday if needed) and go through everything. I promise, getting your stuff together is going to save you when it comes to your ability to get things done. Not to mention, think of how on top of your stuff you'll feel when you walk into the office on Monday morning! The first year of my first job, I spent a few hours over the weekend in the office, just to make sure my desk was cleaned out and organized so that I could perform well the following week. This isn't always necessary but if you are feeling really behind it can be a great idea.

Additionally, don't be afraid to change it up. If you don't like the filing system the last person had, start your own. Make new labels and give everything a refresh. If you can't stand the file folders, go buy new ones, even if it's on your own dime—it will be worth it. Find the processes and organizational systems that work best for you. Make them as intuitive as possible. When you are all done, quiz yourself: Do you know where everything is?

Organize Yourself at Work

Have a workbag that you take with you every day. Something large and black or brown depending on what colors you wear the most. You want to avoid having to change your workbag all the time, losing contents in all the shifting. Keep it organized with all of your work must-haves for the office. Some of the must-haves for your workbag might be:

- cell phone
- extra charger (portable charger)
- wallet (credit cards, at least $20 in cash, ID)
- checkbook (if necessary)
- laptop and charger (if you work from your own computer)
- iPad and charger (if you bring one to work or your company bought you one)
- pens—at least five
- smaller notepad for random ideas that come up (Of course you'll take your work notebook with you to and from work all of the time.)
- business cards (If you have any—many companies don't offer cards until you get that second or third position.)

- vitamins or pills you need to have with you just in case you need to stay at the office late
- scarf or sweater that goes with everything—just in case you are cold or need a quick outfit fix
- deodorant
- perfume or cologne

Create a Calendar System

In my first book, *All Work, No Pay*, I talked about creating an effective calendar system that works for you. The difference now is that you may need to create a system or adapt a system that works for your boss or your superiors in the office. At most companies, you will share a calendar with your team or with your boss—meaning you will have access to their calendar. This is probably the one process that you can't change to your liking because it affects your boss. The majority of employers that I work with are using either Microsoft Outlook calendars or Google Calendar. Both are relatively easy-to-understand tools that you can practice working with before your first day. Also, make sure you figure out how to sync your work calendar to your phone. For example, my Windows Phone automatically uses Outlook, so I had to download a program called Smart Calendar to sync Google Calendar with my phone. Regardless of what type of phone you have, FIO—figure it out.

At my first job we used Outlook calendars to track meetings, calls, appointments, and client schedules. It's so important that everything gets clearly put into the calendar. Put everything in the calendar, even notes and reminders for yourself so you don't forget things. For example, if your boss says, "I want to talk to you at some point about that client," you should schedule time in the calendar to make sure you don't forget to connect with her. Just put a note at the top of the calendar that says "Ask boss about X client." I've found that the busier you get the more helpful scheduling time becomes.

If you know you have a busy week and that randomly on Friday you need to remind your boss to call her doctor, put a note in your calendar for that Friday morning.

Positive Calendar Habits

You want to get in the habit of developing positive calendar etiquette. In chapter two, we talked about the work itself and how to actually schedule things for your boss and coordinate appointments. Here are a few calendar tips for organizing your calendar once you've already entered the information:

• **REVIEW YOUR CALENDAR FIRST THING.** Every morning, I get on the phone with my team between 8:30 and 9:00 A.M. and review the calendar. We all share a calendar and look at every item together. We make sure that nothing is overlapping, that I'm aware of each appointment, and that I don't have to move anything. I use the calendar as a template to plan anything else I know needs to get accomplished that day. I'll even write in when I'm planning on going to the gym or going for a run. Look at your calendar every morning and then again when you're ready to leave for the day. You have to be aware and on top of what's going on with your schedule and oftentimes your boss's schedule. You have to manage the calendar and constantly make sure nothing conflicts. On Fridays, you should look ahead to the following week to make sure you aren't going to walk in on Monday morning and find something completely out of control. You'll want to do the same thing on Monday and make sure nothing has changed.

• **SYNC YOUR CALENDAR WITH YOUR PHONE (FOUND UNDER CALENDAR SETTINGS).** My phone beeps ten minutes before every phone or in-person meeting to make sure I don't forget.

• **KEEP YOUR CALENDAR AS CLEAN AND ORGANIZED AS POSSIBLE.** Enter in as much information as possible so you don't have to look for it minutes before a call or meeting is about to start. Delete old items that are no longer relevant or old reoccurring events that are no longer happening.

Create your own way of organizing.

• **MANAGING YOUR INBOX.** My inbox is insane, constantly. I'm sure you can relate. Every morning I wake up to a mix of everything—author interviews, campaigns to price out, mail from readers, and other seemingly urgent work. And then there is the personal stuff—the group chain e-mails about the foodie restaurants to check out, weekend plans, and LivingSocial deals. My inbox and I have a love/hate relationship. Some days I ignore my inbox all day—I have to spend my time on active or productive work. Other days, I spend all day on my inbox. Here are some ways to manage your inbox:

• **DON'T LET E-MAILS SIT.** When you clean your room, you put everything in its place. Just like cleaning up any other space, e-mails should have their place. If you have e-mails sitting in your inbox that you know you'll never go through, archive them—clear them out—do whatever you can to get them out of there and start fresh. For me, that meant getting rid of my dated Gmail account, which had more than twenty thousand e-mails, and creating an Outlook account for the purpose of getting a fresh start and a clean inbox. If I need to find an old e-mail, I can always log into my old Gmail account and search for it. I'm a big believer in an e-mail filing system. You can file by client, by project, by revenue stream—whatever you want, just file them. Today, I file my e-mails by topic: Book, TV, Clients, Interns, Fan Mail, and Branding Projects. When I go through my e-mail, I feel like I'm cleaning my room, I'm putting every message in its place.

• **DON'T LET YOUR INBOX RUN YOUR LIFE.** It would be easy to end up spending our entire day answering e-mails. Everyone loves to brag about how busy they are and how many e-mails they get. I'll talk more about being "too busy" later in the book. To be honest, I'd be jealous if someone told me they got only ten e-mails a day. While e-mails are great, when we don't use them efficiently they tend to overwhelm us. I like to put as much information as I can in one e-mail and then think ahead, predict the questions the other person might ask, and include that information in the e-mail as well. And realize that sometimes a simple phone call is best for getting the information you need or getting across the information you have. Don't be a slave to your inbox. I try to follow the rules of my e-mail guru, the famous Julie Morgenstern, author of *Never Check E-mail In The Morning*. I focus on a project in the morning before scanning my inbox so that I take control of my day instead of my inbox taking control of it. The thing about e-mails is that there are always going to be more. And they tend to become this growing mountain that you just can't keep up with until one day you are so far behind that you have to devote an entire day to simply managing your inbox—ugh!

• **AVOID E-MAILS AT NIGHT.** Try to avoid work e-mails in the evenings unless it's urgent. I also try to avoid checking my work e-mails from my phone. If I get wrapped up in the wrong e-mail before bed, I can't sleep. Before I leave the office, I scan my to-do list for anything urgent that needs to get done. In my mind, urgent is something that can't wait until the morning that someone is specifically waiting on. For example, today I needed to leave the office by 4 P.M. for a 5 P.M. appointment. It was a heck of a busy day, I quickly scanned my to-do list. There were at least five or six high priority items (items with dollar signs attached) that needed to be completed sooner rather than later. However, there was one other item on my to-do list—it said, "Send payroll to CPA before EOD (end of day)"—that I knew needed to be done ASAP. If I don't send my payroll to my CPA, my employees won't get paid on time. I was able to conquer this task before leaving the office for the night.

• **LIMIT JUNK.** If you've been receiving the same newsletters for years and are just in the habit of deleting every day, click unsubscribe or create a filter that will catch and delete these emails. Only subscribe to the newsletters that you actually read. On my Outlook, I can click SWEEP and my computer will identify mail from specific junk senders and delete everything from that sender in my inbox. This function saves me a ton of time. I'm also able to determine whether or not I want to receive messages from that person again.

• **FILE AND SAVE NEW CONTACTS.** Always add new contacts that you e-mail with and have calls with to Outlook. You want to save their information and sync it with your phone so that you can access their information quickly. You never know when you'll need to quickly access that person's information and you want it in a place that's organized and easily accessible.

• **DON'T FILE UNTIL YOU ARE DONE WITH IT.** Try to look at your inbox as an extended version of your to-do list. Don't file an e-mail until you are done with it. Once you are done with a task, file that e-mail and use the search bar in your inbox to search for any other e-mails related to that task (chain e-mails, group e-mails, etc.). You can hit select all and file them all at once, that way you are removing large quantities from your inbox at once instead of having to go through one at a time.

• **KEEP YOUR PERSONAL E-MAILS SEPARATE FROM YOUR WORK E-MAILS.** My friends and I are on group e-mail chains all of the time. We are very specific regarding which e-mail address we are sending to. My close friend Josh works at Paramount. We don't send personal e-mails to his Paramount e-mail address; we send them to his personal Gmail address. This helps him keep his personal e-mails separated from his work e-mails and makes sure he doesn't get distracted during the day with personal e-mails. And remember, your company technically owns your computer and any work you do from your work e-mail address. It's generally not a great idea to have personal e-mails that your boss could read sitting in your work inbox.

• **USE FOLDERS TO FILE, ORGANIZE, AND ARCHIVE.** Keep as much information as you can. You never know when you'll need to reference an e-mail. Archive your folders on your computer and on an external hard drive. Don't keep everything stored on your phone as it will eat up the memory. Be aware of how many gigabytes you have so you don't start losing e-mails on your phone.

• **UTILIZE YOUR INBOX ORGANIZATIONAL TOOLS.** Most of the time, you won't be able to handle everything that comes across your desk in one day. Prioritize your inbox. Use the color coding system (if that works for you). You could select one color to flag an e-mail to say "this is priority" and others to say "this can wait." Lacey, a former ambassador of mine, who works at Flint Communications, says, "Another cool trick in Outlook is to create rules. I use this for industry newsletters that I'm signed up for. This way, they bypass my inbox and I don't feel obligated to read them right away but I know I can save them for future reference."

Apps to Help You Stay Organized
Including a section on helpful apps wouldn't have been possible if I was writing this book fifty years ago—or even five years ago, but so

many of us are discovering the latest and greatest apps to help us organize our work lives. Here are a few of the most notable apps young people are using in the workplace to stay organized:

- Evernote (https://evernote.com/): Evernote is a phone and computer application for note-taking. On Evernote, I have several notepads, which allow me to take notes and photos while I'm out and about and sync them with my computer.
- Clear (http://www.realmacsoftware.com/clear/): Clear is an organization app for iPhone and iPad users. The tool helps you create simple and easy-to-navigate to-do lists.
- Google Keep (https://drive.google.com/keep/): Google Keep is a tool for note-taking available on Google Play or for Android Users. Many of my Intern Queen followers swear by this tool.
- Trello (http://www.trello.com): Trello is a system of organizational boards on which you can keep to-do lists, track projects, and share it all with coworkers.
- Basecamp (http://www.basecamp.com): Saya, another former ambassador, works at a company called Push in Orlando and says, "On Basecamp you can build your own to-do list for each campaign. It helps separate different jobs that you need to be working on and helps you mark the highest priority."

PRIORIT-IZE
How to Make Sure You Meet Deadlines

Work deadlines are extremely important. Entry-level employees fall on one of two sides of the deadline scale. They either meet their deadlines or they don't. I guarantee, regardless of the excuse, if you don't meet your deadlines, it will affect the way your coworkers and superiors think about you and determine whether or not to give you additional work.

When determining a deadline, give yourself more time than usual. It's better to get something done on time in a way that you can really handle, rather than promising some unreasonable deadline that you are either not going to make or you are going to be late meeting. My literary agent Katie is remarkable at this. We'll have a conversation on a Monday, go over some projects, thoughts, and ideas, and then she will make sure to tell me at the end of our call when I can expect her to follow up on certain things. For example, she'll say, "Great. I'll get that contract reviewed by the end of next week and that call into the publisher in two weeks." At first, my reaction was, "Why can't we do things faster?" I quickly realized, however, that the difference with Katie was that she does what she says she's going to do. I never have to follow up or double check that she's doing it. She simply does things when she plans to and in the manner she is used to. It works. Katie understands her process and knows how long it will take her to complete projects. As you get more comfortable with your workload, you will be able to estimate how long certain projects and tasks will take.

Assign Deadlines When They Don't Exist

When deadlines don't exist you always want to find out what your boss is thinking. Don't just let them blindly assign you work with no structure to it. Go out of your way to ask questions, such as "When would you like me to complete this by?" If they look at you funny, explain that you want to make sure you prioritize and plan accordingly. You can always express the importance of meeting your deadlines if they pry further. Don't be afraid to ask about a deadline. Ask the questions you don't want to ask. It's better to know about a deadline than have your boss assume you know when the deadline is. Also, if you feel overwhelmed and like you have too much on your plate, select the deadline and run it by your boss. Show your boss that you understand your workload by setting your own deadlines. If you need to, you can explain all of the other urgent tasks you are prioritizing.

Once your boss gives you a deadline make sure to look at your calendar and actually plan time to do whatever it is they are asking you to do. It's easy to say you are going to do things, it's another thing to get them done.

Now, let's say someone e-mails you to ask if you can do something. You know it's going to take a long time and you aren't sure when you will do it. Give yourself a deadline and let the person know what the deadline is. Even if it's far out, give them a deadline, stick to it, and manage their expectations.

Some Quick Prioritizing Tips

- Always have sticky notes on hand. If there is something really important that you need to remember to do put a sticky note in the middle of your computer screen. If actual sticky notes aren't your thing, your computer and phone both probably have virtual sticky note organizational systems for you to use.
- Planners: Some people keep their schedules solely online while others still enjoy carrying around a cute planner in their purse (I personally love the Lilly Pulitzer planners). Melinda Price from the Autism Community Network says, "I use my planner to keep a running to-do list, as well as write down all of my appointments and meetings so nothing falls through the cracks. There's nothing more rewarding than checking things off as you go through your day!"
- Always have a notebook with you. They change lives. You should have different notebooks for different projects and parts of your job.

- Make piles of different things on your desk. Try to avoid clutter at all costs.

To-Do Lists

• **LEARN TO PRIORITIZE.** Make sure to go through your to-do list after you put it together and circle anything that should be done first. It's easy to start with the fun stuff that you enjoy, but I suggest starting with the things that you don't want to do. You want to make sure you get these things done and you will most likely get to the things you enjoy regardless. When I write my to-do lists I try to estimate the amount of time it will take me to accomplish that task. This helps me prioritize my list and figure out what I should work on first. Depending on deadlines, I like to tackle the most important projects first to get them out of the way.

• **AVOID DISTRACTIONS AT ALL COSTS.** Find your no-distraction zone where you can get into a rhythm. Do you need to sit in a conference room? Close your door? Shut your cell phone? Put your headphones on? Do whatever you need to do to get to that place where you can rock through your pile of work. When I'm in book-writing mode my e-mails, *The Real Housewives of Beverly Hills*, and friends calling my phone all easily distract me. In order to make sure I'm focused and able to prioritize my time, I shut my phone, sit far away from the television, and shut off my internet connection. I realize that you might not deal with television as a distraction at your office but that doesn't mean there aren't other types of distractions you have to deal with. The point here is do what you need to do to get in the zone.

• **LISTS PRE-BEDTIME.** I find that making to-do lists the night before helps me stay on track first thing in the morning. I write down the five most important things I need to do the next day and usually the time frame that describes how I'll conquer each task. Doing this helps me dive right into my day and get focused faster.

• **MY TO-DO LIST MIRRORS MY INBOX.** I like my to-do list to line up almost perfectly with my inbox. If it's in my inbox, it's probably on my to-do list. If it's in my inbox and not on my to-do list, it SHOULD mean I've completed the task and can delete the e-mail. Remember, you can't let things fall through the cracks. This is a way to double-check that you don't miss things or let them slip.

• **BE FLEXIBLE.** Although I'm clearly obsessed with my to-do list, I must also understand when to be flexible. Being flexible is necessary in your first job and in any fast-paced working environment. Things pop up—such is life. This is just another reason to start with the most important stuff on your to-do list. You want to be organized but not so tied to your ways that you can't be flexible and move some things around. I make a to-do list every night but I guarantee things get changed around several times during the day.

• **COMMUNICATE ABOUT YOUR PROGRESS.** Check your to-do list throughout the day to make sure you stay on track and see what's coming up next. Keep an open dialogue with your boss so that if something is taking you longer than you thought it would they are aware. It's always better to over communicate. Follow up with people about your progress on tasks before they have the opportunity to follow up with you.

MAXIM-IZE

When I was in college I was into making collages. (Now everyone does that on Pinterest.) I would rip out my favorite fashions, slogans, motivational words, celebrity photos, and put them up all over my dorm room. One specific phrase always stuck with me. It said, *Maximize*

Your Potential. I loved it. It impacted me. I felt it. In college, I knew I wanted to do something amazing. I remember sitting by the famous landmark fountain on Florida State's campus (the first college I went to before transferring to UCF) with friends one evening and just looking up at the stars. "I'm going to do something big," I said. "I don't know what it is yet, but I know it's going to happen." It was one of those magic moments that you never forget. And I just remember thinking about that phrase I ripped out of a magazine and taped to the middle of my bed post. "I'm going to maximize my potential."

Maximizing your potential is making the most of your time, being efficient, doing your absolute best on the job every single day. I have a few pointers I'd like to share on how to maximize your potential.

Surround Yourself with People of Similar Mind-Sets

Don't work with people who can't get it done. We all know which people in the office do what they say they are going to do and which people are slackers. When you work with others on assignments, try to partner yourself with like-minded people who take themselves seriously and have a "get it done" mentality. You want to work with people that have a similar work ethic and hold themselves accountable for doing what they say they are going to do. Work with people who maximize themselves in the office every day, who love their jobs, who come in ready to work, who display compassion and humility in the workplace. Work with people who can get the job done. The benefit here will be mutual. Remember the old rule: You are who you associate yourself with.

Build Realistic Goals

Remember, failure is not an option. You are going to maximize yourself every day on the job. You will set goals, decide how to reach those goals, track your progress, and then continue to set higher goals. However, don't set yourself up to fail. Build realistic goals. I'd rather you surpass your goals than fall short of them. Like everything else, it takes baby steps. Meet my friend Ashley. She and her husband just took over a restaurant in Cincinnati, Ohio—the Rail House. The restaurant they took over had a primarily older clientele, and with the new restaurant they are trying to attract a younger crowd. Ashley is in charge of the marketing for the restaurant. She doesn't have a ton of marketing experience but is ready to set realistic goals and give it a try. She eventually wants to pack the house (every night), but knows she needs to start small and build up to her larger goal. She starts out with a few realistic goals for every week: Host at least two parties in the restaurant each week, promote the restaurant to at least five local businesses each week, and personally get to know ten young customers each week (when you have personal relationships with your customers they are likely to return). These were the goals that Ashley started with. Once she accomplishes these goals she will be able to focus on her larger goal—to pack the house every night.

Goal Setting and Tracking

I hear people talk frequently about short-term goals and long-term goals. We all have long-term goals. We want to be millionaires. We want to get married. We want kids, a dog, and a white picket fence. Personally, I want a closet like the Kardashians, a condo overlooking the water, and a Mercedes-Benz G-Class Wagon—yes, it's the one that looks like a milk carton! But what about the long-term goals pertaining to our career? Where do we want to end up? What kind of position do we want? And what about the short-term goals? What do we want to achieve next month, next year, or even tomorrow?

When you start your job, you get thrown in. But a big mistake that first-year employees make is to forget to set goals for themselves. You can easily get so swept up in the madness of your first job that you forget to make goals and keep yourself on track. As I explained in chapter two, a job isn't just something that goes on forever. It has a start date and an end date. It's one leg of your flight; it's part of the puzzle; it's just the starting point of your career. According to the U.S. Bureau of Labor Statistics, the average person stays at their job four years longer than they want to. This is your warning. You can get stuck. Don't get stuck. Have a goal. Have a plan. Typically, once you start in a position and learn the company culture, you'll learn the average time it takes someone to get promoted, and you'll start to notice the "lifers," the people who have been at their jobs forever—some by choice, some not. Take note of the average time and make a goal of getting promoted one month before the average time. Is the first day of your job too early to start thinking about your promotion? No way. At Morgan Stanley, you are eligible for a promotion every eighteen months. As soon as you start a new position, they start preparing you for the series of interviews that will prepare you for your next position. This is a great example of a large company that encourages goal setting regardless of position or rank.

Meghan Maxey, executive store team leader at Target, spoke to me about the importance of young executives continuously setting goals for themselves. "Not only is it important for our execs and leadership teams to set goals for themselves, but it's also important for them to find out the goals of their team members. Once you understand someone's goals, you are better able to understand their motivation."

Examples of Goals to Set Within a Company

- To get promoted to the next level
- To make connections and nurture relationships

- To be aware of your company's or your team's current projects and feel up to speed with the current projects in the office
- To earn your boss's respect
- To demonstrate that you can think outside of the box
- To show that you can be an entrepreneur inside a large company
- To develop a better understanding of the industry
- To read X amount of trade publications about your industry each month
- To be directly responsible for generating X amount of dollars for the company (if this applies to your job) and to bring X number of new projects to the table
- To set up X amount of work-related breakfasts, lunches, dinners, or drinks each month
- To do your job better than anyone else could do it

I use Excel and Google Docs to track my goals. Google Docs are great for easily creating detailed spreadsheets and providing users with the ability to share their information. Multiple people can view a Google Docs file at the same time, so this helps whether you're organizing a project with team members or planning a vacation with friends.

On top of just tracking your goals, you must hold yourself responsible for accomplishing them, constantly coming up with new strategies and having a set of consequences for yourself. If I don't finish filing every paper, what happens? Remember when I spoke about thinking about the consequences before you make decisions in chapter one?

Accountability

We spend so much time setting goals and making to-do lists, timelines, and strategies. But who holds us accountable for achieving these goals? Here are some of the tips I follow to hold myself accountable.

Ways to Hold Yourself Accountable

I suggest finding an accountability partner. Years ago, I met a fellow female entrepreneur, Elizabeth Saunders, now the founder of Real-LifeE.com and author of *The 3 Secrets to Effective Time Investment*, at a speaking conference. Elizabeth and I got along great and one of the things we had in common was that we were both young female entrepreneurs who had just started our own businesses. Elizabeth and I started getting on the phone every other week, talking about our goals and what we wanted to accomplish that week. As accountability partners, we always made sure to check in with each other at the beginning of the call to see if we completed our goals from the week before. Elizabeth and I started doing this in 2010, and four years later, we're still going strong. Even today, when our goals are bigger and have more financial bearing on us, we still need someone to hold us accountable. It doesn't necessarily get easier. But the goal is to create systems to make sure you are able to get things done.

Don't just talk about your goals, take the necessary steps to achieve them. I'm perceived as someone who does what I say I'm going to do. If I hear myself talking about an idea, I immediately follow it up with a calendar note so that I make time for myself to work on that idea. I do this very frequently. For example, I'll tell my Programs and Projects manager, Lindsey, "We need to set a time to discuss X client," and my next sentence is, "Okay, let's open the calendar and actually coordinate a time to discuss that client." If I'm talking about it, I need to make it happen. It's important that my personal brand be one that people can count on no matter what.

Encourage Frequent Evaluations

Most companies do offer yearly reviews where you sit down with your bosses to review your performance and discuss whether or not you get a bonus. I suggest speaking to your boss when you get hired and asking how frequently you will get evaluations or feedback. If you have the opportunity, try setting up evaluations every six months. Regardless of your ability to get a promotion, you want to constantly stay top of mind for your boss, continue an open dialogue about your future inside the company, and get as much constructive criticism as possible. Sometimes, we think we are doing our best at work and our bosses or colleagues think differently—you want to try, as much as possible, to stay on the same page as your boss in terms of your performance.

I've compiled a list of criteria from various entry-level evaluation forms I gathered from both large and small companies. Go ahead and take this mock evaluation and see how you do.

Overall Performance

Evaluations are crucial to your success at a company. If you want to grow within your role (as I believe you all do), you must constantly be evaluated by the company so they watch your progress. Evaluation is also a great individual learning tool. It's very healthy to comprehend how your employer sees your strengths and weaknesses.

General Organization

We talked about overall organization in chapter three. Organization of information usually means you are organized enough to get your job done in a timely manner. Are you able to easily access information? Are your e-mails filed in a systematic way so that you can quickly access information when you need it? Is your work being handled in an organized manner? Are things popping up last minute? Are you prioritizing your work properly? Are things slipping through the cracks?

TIME MANAGEMENT

During your evaluation, time-management skills will be one of the things they look at. Does your employer feel you are on top of your workload? Do you have a solid understanding of your boss's priorities or your company's priorities? Is your boss confident in your abilities to manage a heavy workload and meet your deadlines? Are you completing assignments on time?

PROFESSIONALISM

How do you carry yourself? How do you handle stressful situations? How do you handle rude clients or coworkers? Do you treat everyone respectfully and professionally? How do you carry yourself from day to day?

WORK ETHIC

Do you work hard in your role? Do you show up on time? Work until the job is done? Do you appear passionate? Do you get your tasks completed in a timely manner?

CONTROL OF POSITION

Are you in control of your position? Or is your position in control of you? Are you always a hundred percent aware of the business you have to handle? Are all of your projects and clients under control at all times?

CLIENT MANAGEMENT

How do you work with the clients? How promptly do you handle their concerns and requests? Do you follow up with them frequently enough?

PROJECT MANAGEMENT

Are you effectively managing all of your projects and campaigns? Are you on top of every deliverable? Are you appropriately communicating with the client? Are you keeping your supervisors in the loop regarding the status of all projects? Are you following through with all of your promises?

SAMPLE EVALUATION
- General organization
- Time management
- E-mail organization
- Prioritization
- Solid understanding of company
- Meet deadlines
- Punctuality
- Professionalism
- Mannerisms
- Work ethic
- Follow through
- Control of position
- Detail oriented
- Client management
- Relationship management
- Project management

Raising the Bar and Keeping It Up

My friend Rob (one of the many people I got to meet while in an internship program) is a television writer. Rob started in show business as an agent's assistant (like me) and as a writer's assistant. Rob knows what he is good at and is very aware of his skill set. Two of his greatest strengths are fast typing and detailed note-taking. Rob was taking notes in a meeting one day alongside the show's assistant. At the end of the meeting, the two of them compared notes and Rob's were much more thorough. They were detailed, focused, and easy to read. Rob consistently brought this skill to the table—he took better notes than everyone else 99 percent of the time, and people started to notice. Rob was eventually given the role of being the "official" notetaker. It might not sound like much, but in Hollywood where promotions are one in a million, this was big. Rob then got to be part of every meeting. He would get called into rooms where important decisions were being made. He understood the level of detail the producers were looking for. Because he was in those rooms, Rob was able to build relationships faster than anyone else while simultaneously adding value and creating a lasting impression. He was executing on a regular basis to the best of his ability.

Complacency Kills

I was training at the gym the other day with my trainer, Mo. He's the manager of the entire team of trainers at the gym. I asked him what the biggest mistake is that he sees entry-level trainers make. He laughed at me. "I can't help you with your book. This is a completely different world." I reminded him that workplace advice is more universal than he thinks. Mo said that the number-one mistake he sees is that the new trainers get complacent quickly. They get comfortable. They reach a certain point, then they get lazy and they don't want to try anymore. What a great universal tip for all people in every kind of workplace to hear. You have to fight complacency. Just because it's not the first day, the first week, the first month, doesn't mean it's time to sit around. You should always be setting goals, challenging yourself, and learning new things. The second you catch yourself becoming too comfortable at work, challenge yourself. Give yourself a project. If you can't think of something ask your manager—or your mentor—to give you a special project.

You should constantly be evaluating whether or not you're on the right path to your dream job. Sometimes the job that's right for us at the beginning isn't right for us a few years later. That's what happened to me with my talent agency job. It made sense at the beginning but after two years, I needed to get out of there. I was wasting my time being complacent at work. You want to make sure you don't get stuck. If you stay in the wrong place too long you could burn out or you could get promoted. Now, a promotion might sound amazing but if it's a promotion in the wrong department it could delay your reaching your dream job scenario even longer. When you get offered a promotion in a department that isn't what you really want it's appealing because of the title, the pay, and even the respect you know you'll get in the office. However, a year after the promotion you might be stuck in a job that pays you but makes you miserable. I'd rather you hustle and be happy than make a ton of money and be miserable. Wouldn't you?

Constantly Reinvent Yourself at Work

At any stage in your career, but especially at the beginning, you never want to stop building, creating, trying, and reaching for a goal. Try these steps to keep yourself fresh and inspired at work:

• **GIVE YOURSELF AN EVALUATION.** Time expert and author Laura Vanderkam told me that every January she makes a list of goals for the year and every December she gives herself an evaluation to see how she's done and what she's accomplished. I love this idea! Give yourself an evaluation. Are you reaching your goals? Are you staying focused and motivated at work? Are you continuing to strive for new tasks, responsibilities, and promotions?

• **WHO DO YOU ADMIRE?** Think about the people within your company and outside of your company who you admire or catch yourself saying, "I wish I could be more like _____." What would that person do in your situation? How can you make the most of your current position? What more can you be doing? Make a list of what you come up with.

• **SURF, LOOK, READ.** Read about your industry. What are the trades? Find out what your CEO reads on the weekends. Even if you can't stop what you are doing you can always print that stuff out and read it on the weekends. My first boss would refer to this stack of magazines and interesting articles to take home over the weekend as her "weekend read" pile. I also know people who use the app Pocket to keep track of online articles they come across during the week that they want to read later.

• **STAY CONNECTED AND IN TUNE WITH HIRINGS AND FIRINGS IN THE INDUSTRY.** Make sure to congratulate contacts when they get promoted. You never know what's going to happen—no one is ever as safe as they think they are. Should the worst-case scenario happen and you get let go from your company, you want to feel confident that you are connected enough to find your way. If you follow my work, you know my signature Intern Queen "three times per year" rule, right? My rule is that you stay in touch with your professional contacts three times per year. I'm not in school anymore but I still follow the school year calendar for this rule and get in touch with my professional contacts in the fall, spring, and summer. When you reach out to employers, you just want to drop them a short paragraph telling them how you are doing. Don't ask for anything unless you need to. You want to get in the habit of just reaching out to these contacts so that they don't forget who you are and so when you do need advice, you haven't already tapped out your resource. You also want to stay on top of Facebook groups, LinkedIn groups, Twitter, and more. Chandra, one of my former ambassadors who now works for the start-up 99dresses.com, says, "Keep in touch. I had the opportunity to work with the most amazing people throughout college and in my postgrad years. I make it a point to stay in touch with them, keep them updated on what's going on in my life, and meet up for dinner or coffee whenever possible. My former internship coordinators have introduced me to my future bosses and have offered me invaluable insight. It's great to know I have such a wonderful support system."

Are you done with your *-ize* words for now? Have you had enough? Have I hit the wall of your attention span? Feel free to take a break if you need to but I have plenty more tips and tricks for you in the works. I encourage you to take a moment to think about how you can apply some of my tips related to organizing, prioritizing, and maximizing to your work life—to your real world. I know that you can't implement everything overnight, but try to take one or two of these tips and focus on it tomorrow. Why wait?

CHAPTER 4

How to Work Your Personal Brand

I was watching the MTV VMAs the other night and was fascinated by how each artist behaved during the red carpet, their acceptance speech, and during their performances. You had Miley Cyrus, who was doing everything she could to promote sex appeal and push the envelope. You had Justin Timberlake, who was just brilliant Justin Timberlake—confident, sexy, and, in my opinion, the luxury brand of pop singers. You had Taylor Swift, who portrayed that innocent, classic, girly brand. These artists each represent a different personal brand—and they know how to work their brand. They know how to make sure that every time they are out in public they represent the brand they've worked so hard to create. Everything they did the night of the VMAs was in line with the personal brand they've established in the media. As soon as Miley got out of her car, she stuck her tongue out and started dancing provocatively. Whenever she spoke into a microphone, she continued to provide shock value for the crowd. The same thing went for Taylor Swift (the opposite of Miley), who always dresses and holds herself a certain way. Think of yourself as a business and as a professional brand. What brand do you portray to the public—to the people who aren't your close friends and family? How would they describe your style? How do you carry yourself? Are your actions consistent with your words? Do people know what to expect from you? Do they brand you a certain way in their minds? Is that the way that you want to be personally branded?

People usually maintain two personal brands—one that your family and close friends recognize and another that your business colleagues recognize. In a similar way, I'm sure the professional brand Taylor Swift and Miley Cyrus give off is very different from the way their families know them. For example, if you asked my parents or my close friends about who I am, they would probably say that I'm silly, I can be a baby sometimes, I'm always singing, always eating chicken noodle soup, a solid friend, an aggressive phone caller, and someone who makes things happen.

If you asked someone who works with me in any capacity they definitely wouldn't call me silly or say that I can act like a baby. They would probably say that I make things happen—but as you can see, their perception of my brand is completely different. We have a different relationship. They know my e-mail address. They may have seen my face on a book cover or on Facebook. But that's all they know. I've made sure of that because it's my job to work my personal brand. It's my job to make sure that every time I'm in public, I represent my personal brand in a positive way. Even if it's a Saturday and I'm at the bank annoyed with the teller, I'm going to watch the way I treat that person because I have the "everyone knows everyone" mentality. I assume that someone at the bank might know me in a professional sense or might be familiar with my business. I would never want people to say that the CEO of InternQueen.com and LaurenBergerInc.com yells at her bank teller on Saturday mornings when she's off the clock.

You've all read about having a personal brand before, but in this chapter, I'll explain how to refine that personal brand, manage it, and work it. Regardless of whether you are answering someone else's phone, assisting someone, or acting as a junior executive, you are Your Name, Inc. When I was at the talent agency, every time I opened my mouth, sent an e-mail, or updated a Facebook post, I was adding to (or subtracting from) the Lauren Berger brand. Whenever I walked into the office, I was presenting myself as a specific brand. More important, I was in charge of that brand. I was in charge of what I looked like, how I acted, my work style, and how I carried myself in the office. I was putting a message and a style out into the world and I was in control of how that message came across.

First, I want to dive into refining your personal brand. How does your reputation play into it? How does the way you act at work play into it? Answer the below questions to refine your personal brand:

- Do you treat people respectfully, no matter what?
- Do you showcase a solid work ethic?
- Do you follow your own moral or ethical code?
- Do you hold yourself accountable for your mistakes?
- Do you follow through on what you say you are going to do?
- Do you make others feel comfortable when dealing with you?
- Do you enable others to leave transactions with you and think, "Wow, I'd love to work with that person again"?

    Your reputation is a large part of your personal brand and outlines what others expect from you and don't expect from you. Answering the above questions will help you understand how you might come across to coworkers, clients, and your boss. I encourage you to try to find three adjectives that you think describe your personal brand. Earlier, I described Taylor Swift as innocent, classic, and girly. I would describe the brand I've created for myself as motivational, colorful, and energetic. How would you describe your personal brand? Before you can work your personal brand, you must be able to define it.

THE WAY YOU LOOK

As I've mentioned, the way you dress and your personal style plays into your personal brand. What does your style say about your brand?

In order to work your personal brand you must be able to communicate a professional message through your style. There is a way to express yourself while keeping it professional at work.

How *Not* to Dress at Work

Over the past couple of years, I have talked to executives about Gen Ys in the workplace, trying to find out what young people could be doing better. Over and over again, I heard the same thing: The way they dress. *Casual. Scandalous. Too sexy. Bare shoulders. Leggings. Flip-flops. Expensive jeans with holes.* And: *Bra straps.*

The old saying, "Dress for the job you want, not the job you have," holds true. You have to remember that how you appear plays into your personal brand. I'm not talking about how you naturally look, I'm talking about what you wear, how you dress, how you carry yourself—these are all factors people take into consideration when subconsciously determining your brand. Think about Miley Cyrus and Taylor Swift; both of their styles reflect the brand image they are trying to present to the world. Miley's look tends to be provocative and sexy while Taylor's tends to be more modest and girlish. When you dive into the workplace, it's like starting a clean slate. No one knows who you are or what you stand for. It's a great opportunity to create any personal brand that you want. Every day, when you get dressed for work, you are representing the person you want to be in the workplace. People would argue that if you dress too casually, you are personifying the way you want people to see you and your career path. For example, if you're dressed like you're going to the beach at work (wearing flip-flops), they might think you aren't taking yourself very seriously. You don't need a new outfit every day and you certainly don't need to dress like a rock star but the clothes you do wear need to feel professional and polished and be consistent with the brand image you are trying to project.

How to Dress at Work

- Black jeans are still jeans.
- If jeans aren't allowed don't wear them.
- Ripped jeans aren't allowed. Not even on casual Fridays.
- Leggings aren't workplace appropriate.
- If you could wear your work outfit to a club, you are probably wearing the wrong outfit.
- Mix and match as much as you can. You'll create more outfits than you ever imagined and save money in the process.
- Casual Fridays don't apply to other days of the week.
- Just because it's a nice, button-up blouse, doesn't mean it's OK to wear if it's see-through or has been crumpled in the bottom of your hamper for three days.
- If you could be perceived as the *Price Is Right* model, put a cardigan on it.
- If you look like a naughty secretary, your skirt is too short or your shirt is too tight.
- If any part of your outfit belongs in the book *Fifty Shades of Grey*, take it off immediately . . . and put something else on!
- Hesitant about your outfit choice? Pick another. (Note: If you are hesitant, it's probably not a great sign.)

WAYS OUR GENERATION HARMS THEIR PERSONAL BRAND AT WORK
Acting Entitled

Gen Y has a bad reputation. They are called entitled, the trophy generation, the microwave generation, and the list goes on. We know that, by and large, this isn't true. But how can we avoid falling into these stereotypes? Be humble. Learn to be grateful for your situation.

If you act entitled, no one will want to go out of their way for you. Don't say things like "I deserve to make more money" or "I'm above this task." When you are an entry-level employee, no task should be too small; you should volunteer and eagerly do the work no one else wants to do in hope that people will recognize your genuine spirit. Another former ambassador of mine, Alicia Valko, works at Jack Morton. She says, "I am humble and understand that I am an entry-level employee—not the CEO. I'm careful not to be seen as entitled." And Alicia's right—this is very important in today's working society.

Being Inconsistent

Your job is to be consistent. To set the bar somewhere and keep it there. Did you do an outstanding job on one project? Great! You've now set the standard. You are now expected to do an outstanding job on every project. Can it be difficult to perform in an environment with high expectations? Yes, but who said work was easy? And it's not just your actual work. Your attitude, work ethic, organization, prioritization, and maximization should all be consistent. Once you make an impression, you must make it last. Consistent people get ahead. For example, if you are usually in a great mood, be in a great mood every day. If you are usually willing to help people out in the office, always be willing to help people out. People will appreciate your consistency and that consistency will translate into reliability. The best way to get people on your team is by proving that they can rely on you and that you are consistent. This is a great way to brand yourself.

Surfing during Work Hours

Here is the thing. Reputations stick. The old saying that you don't get a second chance to make a first impression holds true. So if people see you hanging out on Facebook or online shopping during the day, they'll remember. You are automatically labeled as the person who doesn't have enough work to do, is slacking off, or just doesn't care. You want to make sure that if you have voids in your day you ask for more responsibilities and let your supervisor know. You have plenty of time to "surf" in your spare time. It's not only bad for your boss to see you surfing online but if your coworkers, who might be overworked and tired, see you slacking off they might start to act bitter toward you.

Remember, you are a business inside of a business. The way you act matters, the personality, the attitude—it all matters. You are your own business and people are going to remember what it's like dealing with you. If they didn't like it, they aren't going to want to work with you in the future.

WORKING YOUR SOCIAL CHANNELS

Trying to keep up with our social networks is a full time job in and of itself. I get it. If you have a presence on more than one social network, which I'm sure most of you do, it can be impossible to keep up with. Every morning, I log in to my Facebook and Twitter to scroll the feeds, answer messages and direct replies, and post something clever. Every time I get a LinkedIn notification it goes to my inbox so I approve all of those. I stopped doing Pinterest a few months back as it was just too much to manage. Whenever I'm on my phone, I'm scrolling Instagram and posting fun pictures from my day. Some of my close friends also use SnapChat, Tumblr, and Google Circles. I can't imagine adding another network! In this section, I'm going to run through all of the must-have social media networks and provide you with tips on how to use them the most effectively to maximize your personal brand. Luckily, I've met some amazing young people over the years and I spoke with the author of *Promote Yourself: The New Rules for Career Success*, social media expert Dan Schawbel, to get some further insight into what you can do today to work your professional brand online. In the below sections, I incorporate his tips with mine.

Our generation knows how to use social media like none other. In fact, one of the reasons you are going to land jobs over other people is because you know how to integrate social media into your life in unique ways—ways that companies are interested in learning about. So what's the real deal here? What social networks do you need to know how to use for any job? What social networks will set you apart and how can you utilize them to help you do so?

How to Work Your Brand via Facebook

- **CLEAN UP THE JUNK AND VALUE PRIVACY.** Take down the drunken photos, the revealing photos—basically any photos you wouldn't want your employer to see.

Delete the strange comments your friends write on your wall that can be interpreted in the wrong way. And yes, even the bikini photos get deleted! Bikini profile pictures or other inappropriate photos are not okay on your social media sites. Does your employer really need to see you like that? Do your coworkers need to see that?

Many recent grads ask me if they should keep two Facebook pages—one for their friends and one for their professional profile. In fact, many students already do this; they have one Facebook page (their first name and last name) for their personal friends and another with their first name and middle name for employers. I don't think two Facebook accounts is necessary. You have to have the "everyone knows everyone" mentality. Even if an employer isn't friends with you on Facebook or can't see your profile because it's private, what if someone that they are friends with is friends with you? What if they see that you have some friends in common? You have to assume that the wrong people will come across these photos. Dan Schawbel and I both agree that this is a huge issue with Facebook. Dan says, "More and more recruiters are going to be looking at your Facebook profile. Make sure they are only seeing what you want them to see." This does not mean that changing your privacy settings is all you need to do. You have to assume that people can find things if they are looking. Only post pictures that are appropriate for everyone to see.

• **DECIDE WHO YOUR AUDIENCE IS GOING TO BE.** Dan had a great point here. He says, "Facebook is a complicated network. Our research shows that the average Millennial is connected to an average of seven hundred friends and sixteen coworkers. Before you start adding coworkers into the mix you need to decide who your audience is going to be. Once you start adding coworkers, the content has to change. Posting the wrong kind of information and sharing it with the wrong audience can lead to coworkers feeling isolated or treating you differently."

• **DECLUTTER YOUR FEED.** You don't have to unfriend people you don't care about but hide their feeds so that you can stay up-to-date with the people you do care about. This applies to both your personal and professional life. If you do find it appropriate to friend coworkers or former bosses it will be useful to keep up with what they are doing on Facebook. If there's too much junk in your feed, you might miss the important information.

• **NO ONLINE BASHING.** Don't talk smack about your job or complain that it's almost Monday on your Facebook wall. Nobody will want to hire you if they see that you've had a history of complaining publicly about your positions.

• **NO FRIEND REQUESTS.** Don't friend your employer unless he requests you (at that point you can assess the situation and confirm or deny).

• **CHECK THE COMPANY PAGE.** Make sure you are up to date with your company's Facebook page and check it regularly, it's important to be in the loop on company events.

• **UPDATE IT WITH THINGS THAT YOU ARE INTERESTED IN.** Dan says that if you are going to use your Facebook profile in a professional way, post things that will be relevant or interesting to members of your industry or field. Let a certain amount of your personality shine through on your social media channels. People need to know that you have a voice and you aren't just another working robot. Update your "likes" with your favorite music, movies, and books to give people a look into your hobbies and interests.

How to Work Your Brand via Twitter

• **FOLLOW ALL POTENTIAL TARGET EMPLOYERS ON TWITTER.** Follow both their personal profile pages and their company pages. If you can't follow them regularly, pick one day per week and check in on everybody. Read the news links they tweet and get an idea of their tone and personality via Twitter. If they ask questions, interact. You don't need to have a second Twitter profile. Use one Twitter profile to showcase your personal and professional interests and keep it Rated G.

• **USE TWELLOW.**com. Dan Schawbel is a huge fan of this search site. He encourages young people at work to "search for people in your industry and in your profession that you can follow."

• **MAKE A PRIVATE LIST CALLED DREAM JOBS AND FOLLOW EVERYONE.** You could also make a list called Current Company and follow any staff members that you've found on Twitter.

• **REMEMBER, YOU CAN'T TWEET ANYTHING INAPPROPRIATE.** You can't write anything inappropriate about your job, people who work with you, or the way you feel about going into work unless it's positive.

• **JOIN TWITTER CHATS.** Several of the recent grads in my network rave about how helpful Twitter chats are. Dan Schawbel agrees. "This is something very popular for online networking. Start following different hashtags that are relevant to your interests and try to find the Twitter chat that's perfect for you," Dan says. "Once you find something you like review the conversation, look at the background of the people in the chat, look over the context of the chat, and if you are comfortable—join in!"

• **HAVE AN APPROPRIATE BIO.** Melinda Price (from The Autism Network) points out that your bio matters. She says, "Keep in mind that your bio goes a long way. For example, my bio reads 'Nonprofit marketing, PR enthusiast, content creator, trivia seeker, book lover, future traveler, Miami U alumna, proud Millennial, & downtown San Antonian.' People who choose to follow me know a little bit about what I have to offer on my Twitter feed right off the bat."

• **USE TWITTER AS A PROMOTIONAL TOOL.** Bianca, one of our former ambassadors who just landed her dream job at Atlantic Records in Los Angeles, says, "I'm always tweeting to promote my work, and I also use it to keep up to date on news, music trends, and the daily happenings of my friends." She says that she always thinks twice about her tweets and asks herself, "Does the world really need to know this about me? Would someone negatively judge me by this tweet?"

How to Work Your Brand via LinkedIn
• **FIND DREAM COMPANIES.** Use LinkedIn to look up dream companies or the company you currently work for and see if anyone in your network knows people there.

• **TRACK ALUMNI.** You can also use LinkedIn to see if people from your college work at a certain company (this is a great way in).

• **USE LINKEDIN TO BUILD OUT AND UPDATE YOUR RÉSUMÉ.** The paper résumé can only be one page while the LinkedIn résumé can be as long as you want.

• **JOIN GROUPS.** Joining LinkedIn groups is extremely important as it helps you group yourself with others who have similar titles and interests. Look at some of the executives in your industry that you follow and determine which groups they are part of and then try to join them.

• **EMBRACE THE PROFESSIONAL EXPERIENCE.** Use LinkedIn to professionally brand yourself, it should speak volumes of your professional experience.

Cat Pylant works for WilsonHCG RPO, a recruiting firm, as a second-year employee, and she says, "I use LinkedIn a lot. I'm involved in a lot of different LinkedIn Groups and try to stay involved in the discussions. If I meet someone at an in-person networking event I always add them on LinkedIn as soon as possible."

How to Build Your Brand via Instagram

• **BE CONSISTENT.** Make yourself a goal of uploading at least two to three photos per week on Instagram, utilizing hashtags to see how much engagement they generate. As I mentioned, many companies are running Instagram campaigns so this is a great tool to be familiar with. You can post pictures from when you're out with friends but make sure they are in good taste. If your employer starts to follow you, which isn't a bad thing, you don't want them to have to unfollow you because they are uncomfortable with the photos you are posting.

I had a former intern start posting pictures of her and her boyfriend making out and it made me very uncomfortable. I had to unfollow her because I didn't want to look at her feed anymore. The second I unfollowed her I was removed from her daily happenings and she was no longer top of mind.

• **FOLLOW TARGET EMPLOYERS AND BRANDS.** Similar to Twitter, you should try to follow someone's company feed and personal feed. However, if you have to request to follow someone's personal feed, I would suggest just sticking with the company feed so they don't feel like an employee is stalking them. If they friend you, that's another story.

How to Work Your Brand via Pinterest

With Twitter, Facebook, and Instagram you need to work hard to keep these platforms updated, but with Pinterest you can just use it personally. I suggest creating at least one pin board for yourself. Many students have career-related Pinterest boards with motivational quotes, photos, et cetera, but employers aren't necessarily looking at these boards. They are fine to keep public and fine to continue using as most boards likely won't play much of a role in your hiring decision unless you are going into a very visual field or the fashion or design world.

Bianca from Atlantic Records says, "Pinterest has a far longer impact period, meaning that people may come across your pins months after they've been posted, unlike Twitter, which has a short window for impressions. It's in your best interest to post things on Pinterest that you would feel comfortable posting months in the future and not something that could ever tarnish your reputation. It's often difficult to maintain professionalism on social media while attempting to display your personality, but it's definitely possible to express your interests and passions in a way that boosts your professional brand."

You see, while a job is temporary, your personal brand sticks with you—regardless of what professional opportunity you are trying out at the moment. And by shifting the way you think about your personal brand on a daily basis, you can strongly affect the power of your own. Your personal brand is something you always need to think about and it will constantly be a work in progress. As you develop in your career, you will continue to further the definition of your own personal brand. As you continue to read this book, remember that your reputation, the way you dress, the way you carry yourself, and the way you manage and express yourself through your social networks all play an important role in establishing your brand at work. The most important lesson here is that just because you aren't the CEO of the company doesn't mean you aren't held accountable for representing your company and yourself. You have the power to control your personal brand—so work it.

CHAPTER **5**

Relationships and Schmoozing

At my first job everyone always wanted to go to lunch—it was the weird-est thing. I mean, in college my friends and I would go to lunch but it wasn't a big production. We didn't schedule it over numerous e-mail chains or over the phone. It just sort of happened. And before I knew it I was schmoozing all over the place. I had lunches scheduled, drinks scheduled, dinners scheduled, I had everything scheduled. I mean, we were all trying to act like our bosses. Our bosses were important agents who had meeting with superstars, directors, and producers—we had to at least *try* to sound as cool. And trust me, you were only cool if your calendar was booked months out. If you weren't "really busy" you just hadn't figured it out yet.

Now, the invitation to lunch was just part one. The main purpose of these lunches was so that some assistant whose boss represented Reese Witherspoon could look at you and say, "So Lauren, tell me what you really want to do. What's your plan?" And that was it. The purpose of your lunch. It was politics. They wanted to know your plan so they could use it against you and try to navigate their own. I know this must sound very negative but you have to understand. When you pick up and move your life to Los Angeles, from lord knows where, you get immediately submerged into a pond of wannabes. And whether you want to admit it or not—you are one of those wannabes.

The only problem is that at that point you don't know what you want to be yet. So you fall into the flow, do what everyone else does, and you innocently talk about your plan or whatever some other assistant told you they think your plan should be. The truth is, you most likely have no idea what you are talking about. You tell the assistant that your plan is to excel at your job and then get promoted at the first possible opportunity. You also share which department you'd like to get a promotion within. This supposed "friend" tells everyone your plan. When you finally go to lunch with the next douche from the catalog you hear your plan second hand and think, "Was that really my plan?"

When you break up with your boyfriend, people say things like, "Men are like buses and you just need to wait until the next one comes around." Well, at my first job, *friends* were like buses—every day a new one came by the stop. The problem was these "friends" weren't genuine; once they learned who I was and (probably through gossip) that I wasn't very good at my job, they weren't really interested in talking to me anymore. And it hurt my feelings. I didn't understand the relationships happening around me because I hardly understood myself. We had just graduated college. Our minds, lifestyles, and bodies were changing and transitioning and it was a lot at once. We weren't just on our own for the first time but we also had our first jobs and our first new set of friends. We didn't know what we were doing and that was reflected in our relationships. I wanted to call this chapter networking, but I *hate* the word networking—it just sounds so fake. Why spend time building fake relationships with people when you could spend your time building genuine relationships with them? When I ran the title by my friend Shannon, she screamed. "No!" she said. "I *hate* that word!" That made two of us.

Call it what you want—schmoozing, chatting, connecting, scheming, stalking—relationship building is necessary in the workplace. I mean, how many times have you heard someone say, "Oh, I got that job because my brother's sister's friend's cousin's rabbi was looking for someone?" It happens all of the time. Networking is a necessary part of our work life equation, but relax—we all have a little schmoozer inside of us. We just have to find them.

This chapter is the largest in the book—and rightly so! Relationships are arguably the most important part of the workplace. In this chapter, we'll cover office politics, relationships with your boss, with your coworkers, how to handle working with people you hate (I know, this happens), how to find mentors within your company, dating in the workplace, and some rules to follow on the art of . . . well, let's call it *schmetworking*.

RELATIONSHIPS
POP: Petty Office Politics

The point of this book isn't to teach you how to play games, be nice to certain people, be catty in the office, and participate in POP (petty office politics). I don't want you to leave this book ready to backstab, lie, or mislead people to get ahead. In chapter one, I talked about the ways that I've come to be successful and my recipe for success. One of those points was about attitude. I truly believe that you don't need to be bitchy, spiteful, sneaky, or play politics to get ahead. At the same time, you can't be blind to office politics. They exist—in almost every company of every size. The odds of successfully navigating them are small and completely depend on the company, the relationships, the personalities, and the executives themselves. Here are a few universal tips I can offer on how to deal with POP:

• **UNDERSTAND RELATIONSHIPS.** I want you to be friendly with as many people as you can at the office—not in a fake networky way, but in a real genuine way. Be aware of who knows who and how they know each other. Are they related? Did they meet at work? Did they work together at another firm before this one? Are they personal friends?

Are their husbands friends? Understanding other people's relationships might provide insight into why certain things happen at work. For example, if your boss's husband is best friends with another executive's husband, they might be playing nice for the sake of their relationship outside of the office. They don't want to have a work issue that will harm their personal relationship or their husbands' relationship. Usually people will openly share this information with you. Make sure you are aware of who is friends with who, and how those friendships came to be.

• **KEEP A WATCHFUL EYE.** Be observant. Watch how decisions are made in the office. Watch how promotions are determined. Pay attention to who is getting promoted. If you feel like there might be an unfair situation in the office keep a close eye on how it gets handled. This will also give you insight into the office politics and make you aware of them should you ever be directly involved.

• **CREATE ALLIES.** I've already shed some light on the value of building strong relationships. Over time, naturally establishing a group of people who would go to bat or stick their necks out for you is what you want. You want to build a support team within your office of people who ultimately have your back. This will help you if you're ever in the middle of a game of POP.

• **BE THE BEST FRIEND.** I talked to my friend who works in the entertainment industry about his first job as an assistant on a TV show. I asked how he navigated the office politics. He said, "When I was an assistant on shows, I'd make myself available to people at my level and above me. Whenever they needed someone to talk with, vent to, or run ideas by—I made sure I was there. This enabled me to build strong relationships with a majority of my coworkers and superiors. When people didn't like each other or gossiped about others, I made sure to listen but not to join in. Most of those people still trust me and speak with me today. These strong relationships, years later, enable to me to quickly get information whenever I need it. And I've maintained some pretty great friendships, too!"

• **WATCH YOUR OPINIONS.** Be careful about expressing your opinions at work—especially about clients in the office. You never know who knows who and you never know how much work was put into something behind the scenes and who your negative comments might be affecting.

• **DON'T GET WRAPPED UP IN IT.** Don't gossip. If you observe gossip, be aware of what people are saying but don't participate in it. If someone hears you talking about someone else, they will never trust you. They will always think you are capable of doing the same thing to them.

• **WATCH THE DRINKING.** If you're reading this book, you are most likely over the age of twenty-one and maybe having casual after-hours drinks with coworkers for the first time. It's okay and can be a good thing to go out with coworkers and get cocktails. Just make sure you don't get drunk with your coworkers and cross the line between appropriate and inappropriate. Remember, these aren't people you are meeting out and never going to see again. You have to see them tomorrow morning, so watch how much alcohol you consume and your words and your actions. Know your personal limit (note: this does not mean know how much alcohol you can drink before vomiting). I suggest having one or two drinks max at a work function.

Relationships with Your Boss

At my first job, which I described to you at the beginning of this book, I wasn't very good at what I was doing—I just wasn't—and I can admit that. People always ask what my relationship is like with that very first boss today. And you know what? It's actually pretty great. We see each other a few times throughout the year—usually at personal events like birthday parties and holiday parties. And yes, she has told me that she's very proud of the professional woman that I've become. Today, we can laugh at what a horrible assistant I was and how I still wake up some mornings afraid I might get a phone call from her new assistant asking me about a missing travel receipt.

As I've shared, my first job wasn't easy. There's one story that demonstrates how I handled my inner battle with my first job—by literally driving to my boss's house over a weekend. As you read, I was trying hard (for the most part) and messing up constantly at my first job. One weekend, I decided I couldn't take it anymore. I admired my boss and liked my job. I was just terrible at it. I wanted to be better but knowing that I was walking on eggshells and could get fired any minute wasn't helping. I felt constantly stressed. And so I decided to make a move. A bold move. A move I'm proud of when I think about it. I texted my boss and said, "I'm coming over. I need to talk to you about something. Meet me at Starbucks?" I made her schedule so I knew she was at home reading scripts all weekend. I got in my car, drove to the Palisades where she lived, and met her at Starbucks. She probably thought I was dying or something. I mean, what a weird thing for your assistant to call you and say she's coming over and then drive to where you live. But we sat down—and we talked. I told her that I knew I wasn't doing that well at the job. I told her I loved working for her and I wanted to get better but I didn't know how. I asked her for advice, about her personal experiences, and I told her I needed help. I wanted to get better but felt like I couldn't because I thought she was going to fire me every ten seconds. I was nervous about what her response would be to all of this, but it went really well. She actually applauded my courage and bravery and said, "Wow. You must have been nervous to come and talk to me." I relaxed a bit after that comment. She sat with me for about an hour and gave me some advice, told me her own assistant horror stories, and reassured me that she wasn't going to let me go. She was stuck with me and I was stuck with her for at least a little while. This conversation didn't change everything, but it definitely helped.

Your boss today should be someone that you are in touch with for the rest of your life. Sure, you will work for this person—probably for a short time, maybe a year or two—but you are building a relationship for the bigger picture. You never know how this person will play a part in your life, who they will put you in front of, or the job opportunities they could lead you to. You want to have people in your life who can speak highly of you, talk about your professional capabilities, who can recommend you, and your boss can potentially be that person for the rest of your life.

I started an internship program at my company, Intern Queen Inc, in 2009. At this point, I've gone through several cycles of interns and I'm still in touch with a lot of them. I'm frequently responsible for evaluations, recommendations, writing letters, or making calls on their behalf. And you know what? I'm happy to do it. Here are some tips on handling your relationship with your boss:

• **THEY CHANGE OVER TIME.** Your relationship with your boss today isn't necessarily going to be the relationship you have with your boss a few years from now. Don't get too hung up on the current relationship. When you work for someone the relationship is always going to be intensified. Eventually, you will both move on and the relationship will develop accordingly. Do your best and don't get too hung up on what the relationship will look like five years from now.

• **RECOGNIZE THAT YOUR RELATIONSHIP WITH EVERY BOSS WILL BE DIFFERENT.** Some will be great and others not-so-great—it's typically a personality thing. Some bosses are going to notice some things about you and others will notice other things. Your personality might rub one boss the right way but another boss another way. Such is work life.

• **DON'T LET YOUR BOSS'S MOOD BUG YOU.** The best thing you can do is be consistent—personality wise and work wise. Some people are moody. You can't change who someone is. Be aware of your boss's mood and then go on with your day like normal. The best thing you can do for your boss's mood is act as you normally do. Be the consistent force they can rely on. Don't let your boss's mood affect you. You have no idea what they are dealing with after hours.

• **DON'T WAIT FOR PRAISE.** Whenever people tell me they are waiting for praise, it feels immature to me. Why does someone need to tell you that you are doing a good job? Why can't you be confident in the work you are putting out into the world? Some people get so caught up in waiting for praise that they get frustrated when the accolades don't come around frequently. Be confident in your abilities. Your boss isn't a mind reader and remember, you are expected to do a good job and to do your work—that's part of the job description.

• **IF YOU'RE GOING TO TAKE OFF WORK . . .** Try to provide as much advance notice as possible when going out of town or taking days off. Let your boss plan for this as much as possible and of course, only take sick days when really needed. Successful executives need reliable consistent people who aren't going to take advantage of their time.

• **GET TO KNOW YOUR BOSS'S COMMUNICATION STYLE.** One of our former ambassadors, Dalida, who now works at FindLaw.com (a Thomson Reuters company), says, "For me, one of the hardest parts of my first job was understanding everyone's communication style. There are people who explain everything flat out and there are those who don't explain anything. There are people who ask for something the day they want it and there are people who ask for things days in advance. It just takes some getting used to. It takes time to learn how everyone functions." When you start a new job, ask your boss about their preferred communication methods and styles. When you have questions should those be handled over the phone, in person, via e-mail, or by text?

• **GET IN BEFORE YOUR BOSS.** I've talked to several executives who all say that it's a great feeling to walk into work every day and see the same person sitting there—day after day. These busy executives need someone to rely on, someone to depend on. The more trust they build with you, the more projects they will send your way. When you are a consistent face that your boss sees in the morning and can rely on to be there already running the show that is a great thing. It will also give you time to prepare for what the day brings.

• **DON'T LEAVE THE OFFICE BEFORE YOUR BOSS LEAVES.** Leaving before your boss doesn't set a great precedent. Just sit tight, get organized, and work on tomorrow's to-do list or work pile. If you're out of tasks to do, read the industry trades—make the most of your time in the office. You don't want your boss to come out of his or her office and see you on Facebook regardless of whether it's after 6 P.M.

• **YOU DON'T NEED TO BE BEST FRIENDS WITH YOUR BOSS.** They don't need to know everything about you or your personal life. Unless your boss sends you a friend request, don't be Facebook friends. It's okay to follow your boss on Twitter as it's not as intimate a network as Facebook. It's also okay for you to follow them on Instagram if their profile is public. I would wait a good six months before requesting them as a LinkedIn contact. And just be careful: You would like to avoid a situation where you're supposed to take work home over the weekend, you forget to do it, and your boss sees photos of you and your friends getting wasted at the Malibu Winery all weekend.

• **EMPOWER YOUR BOSS.** Make him or her look good. We'll explore this more in chapter seven on entrepreneurship, but think about what you can do to make your boss look great.

• **PICK YOUR BATTLES WISELY.** There will come a time when something happens and you need to confront your boss. I think we all one day get to that point in our early careers. But you can't pick every fight. You can't have a new bone to pick with your boss every day. Think long and hard about the battles you want to pick and if these battles will be worth it in the long run. Some people start talking back and arguing with their bosses and then they can't stop. At the end of the day, this is your boss—not your friend. It's work. Don't take it personally.

• **BE LOYAL TO YOUR BOSS AND YOUR BOSS WILL BE LOYAL TO YOU.** (We hope!) Try not to keep secrets (work-related) from your boss. Let them know that you are on their side. If you are ever in a situation where people are bad-mouthing your boss, let him or her know. This will help your boss to trust you and know you are to be trusted. Should you expect this loyalty back? Hard to answer, it really depends on the person.

You want to have a solid, long-term relationship with your boss. If nurtured properly, this relationship will last a lifetime and you will forever have this person in your court and on your team. Many of my friends, peers, and colleagues have their former bosses negotiating contracts for them, putting them up for jobs, and supporting them throughout their careers.

Relationships with Your Coworkers

Coworkers can be annoying, competitive, jealous, and better at their jobs than you are. They can also be supportive and understand your situation better than anyone else. Every relationship with every co-worker is going to be different. You will probably hate some, like some, love some, and want to get rid of some—again, such is work life.

When I had my first job, I was the second assistant, meaning that I handled several of my boss's more personal needs. At one point in my tenure at the agency, there was a girl named Rori who was the first assistant. Rori was gorgeous and had the coolest shoes I'd ever seen. Her shoes were Prada—mine were Target. Rori was uber-organized and in that sense, she was everything I wasn't. I always describe her as the kind of person who cares if the rubber band is kept in the rubber band drawer. I'm the kind of person who could sit at my desk and swim in a sea of rubber bands and probably not even notice. As you might imagine, she couldn't stand me. My laid-back style killed her. She was so put together and organized and I'm sure it looked like a giant explosion took place everywhere I went. Looking back, Rori and I had a funny relationship—I think on a personal level we actually enjoyed each other's company, but we just spent so much time in that damn workplace together that she slowly started to hate me. It doesn't need to be like this. Here is how you can deal with coworkers:

• **BE AWARE OF RELATIONSHIPS WITH COWORKERS AND THE INFORMATION THAT YOU SHARE.** Coworkers are work friends (sometimes they do turn into personal friends) and you must make sure you are aware of these relationships. These people are part of your work life, and you want to make sure that if you are going to confide in them about something work-related they aren't going to tell other coworkers who they might be "friendly" with.

• **DON'T BE AFRAID TO GET TO KNOW PEOPLE.** First or second jobs can have a high school feel. It's lunchtime and everyone scurries around trying to secure a table with a "cool group" in the cafeteria. Let me tell you something in all seriousness: NO ONE CARES. For real. Get over it and sit with whoever you want. Be the person that goes up to people you want to chat with or get to know and say, "Hello, can I join?" Remember, you are going to be spending more than eight hours a day with these people! You want to try enjoying their company.

• **DON'T BURN BRIDGES.** People that might be below you on the company hierarchy or those who work at your level now might be your boss later. Trust me, you never know where people will end up. So keep in good graces with everyone and it could prove to be very useful in a few years.

• **EVERYONE HAS A PLAN AND AN AGENDA.** Whether or not they say it out loud, everyone has a plan for themselves within a company. Perhaps they want to get promoted or they want to put in a few years and then move to another company. Maybe it's not that very day, but everyone wants to go somewhere, and you have to be aware that they are following the agenda that is best for them, not you. I told you about my "lunches" at the beginning of this chapter where everyone wanted to ask about my plan. Ultimately, other people's plans don't directly affect you in the workplace. Just remember that people typically have their agendas as a first priority so they are going to do whatever it takes to follow their agenda, not to help you.

• **DON'T TALK ABOUT PAY.** You are only going to upset yourself if you talk with coworkers about what they make. This is the oldest rule in the book. Remember, there might come a day when you are making more than your coworker so don't put yourself in the same awkward situation. If there is a discussion that needs to be had about your salary or income—have that conversation with HR. Don't compare bonuses, gifts, or paychecks.

Find a Mentor

Some companies are great at promoting mentorship programs, others are not-so-great. Try to find a mentor within your company— someone who you can casually speak with about your job and someone who you trust. Some of the most successful people have learned from a mentor at their company.

Mentors can be of great assistance to a young person (or a not-so-young person) navigating the workplace for the first time, trying to grow within a business, and can help when problems or challenges arise. A mentor can also be great in terms of providing you with advice when you think it's time to move on to a different job or help you reinvent yourself within the company when you are feeling stuck. Hopefully, your mentor also keeps you top of mind when he or she is out networking and meeting new people. In my section in chapter one about rejection, I told you the story about my pitch to Ford that got rejected several times but finally got picked up. Well, the guy responsible for that campaign is Lee Jelenic. Today, he runs the global brand strategy for the Lincoln brand. Lee and I worked closely together on the Ford campaign and we always had (and continue to have) insightful business conversations. In a business sense, we just sort of click. Even though we work in different types of environments, we think in similar ways and we learn from each other every time we connect. In fact, he's become a mentor of mine along the way.

After speaking to Lee countless times over the phone (about our Ford deal), I finally had the opportunity to sit down with him. I was in Illinois for the final part of the Ford campaign and we spoke about the progress we'd made. One thing I remember him saying was that he was lucky enough to find a mentor at Ford to sort of pave the way for him. I was shocked! Wow! A company as large as Ford Motor Company has a mentorship program? Who would have thought?!

• **THE BIGGER THE COMPANY, THE MORE IMPORTANT A MENTOR CAN BE.** Lee says that even though it might be harder to find mentors in larger companies, it's even more important. The reason is that big companies tend to have many complicated processes, governance structures, and functions. Early in a career, without the benefit of experience and an internal network, a mentor can be a critical resource in explaining how to efficiently navigate through the various divisions and processes to deliver a project. They can also provide context for an organizational structure or approval process from a higher level in the company. A new hire in their first few years may not see how everything is connected and how different functions interact, a mentor can help make sense of that.

• **GET RID OF YOUR AGENDA.** When you graduate college and get hired at a company your thought process shouldn't be, "Who can further my career the fastest?" Lee explains that when selecting mentors you want to choose someone with no underlying agenda. You want to choose someone who can be a sounding board for you and someone you can be comfortable speaking with.

• **YOUR MENTOR SHOULDN'T BE YOUR MANAGER.** I was surprised to hear this but once Lee explained I completely understood. "You can have a strong relationship with your manager, but there is inherently an underlying agenda with your manager. You work for that person. You are responsible for delivering assignments and projects to that person." You should pick someone who doesn't have an agenda.

• **LOOK OUTSIDE OF YOUR REPORTING CHAIN.** Lee explains that there is a definite upside to selecting mentors outside of your chain of command. "When you have a mentor outside of your reporting chain, their focus can be on your development, to help you grow as a young professional." Lee spoke to me about the importance of finding someone outside of your reporting zone but still someone who's shared similar experiences or positions. "You watch people," says Lee. "And no matter how large the company is—people's personalities come through. Try to select the person that you think you can relate to and think can relate to you."

• **MENTORS DON'T NEED TO BE AT THE TOP OF THE CHAIN.** Lee said that another mistake he's seen young people make in regards to finding mentors is they go straight to the top. But often times, this is too far up the chain. "People gravitate toward more senior people," says Lee. "If your mentor is too senior—especially early in your career—they'll be too far removed from the challenges you are facing and won't be able to offer as much tangible advice. If your mentor is in middle management, their experiences at your level will be more recent and they'll be able to draw on those to offer better advice." Lee points out that having a senior mentor isn't a bad thing, it's just that by and large you won't get as much out of it in your early career. That's the gist.

• **THE RELATIONSHIP IS A TWO-WAY STREET.** Your relationship with your mentor shouldn't be one-sided. When I asked Lee about the mistakes he saw young people making in terms of developing a relationship with their mentors he said, "They tend to make it about themselves. I encourage young people to get to know their mentors and hear about their experiences and how they got where they are." Lee explained that he has taken two full sessions with his mentor just to hear and learn about his mentor's experiences.

• **CREATE YOUR MENTORSHIP PROGRAM.** If your company doesn't have a mentorship program, see if you can help to create one. I asked Lee what advice he has for young people who want to start a program or find a mentor at a company that doesn't have something like this in existence. Lee instructs young people to approach others they think would make great mentors and say, "I know we don't do this yet at our company but I really think I could use a mentor at this stage in my career." If you are feeling ambitious and looking to earn some recognition for going above and beyond your job, you could look into creating a larger scale mentorship program. In today's workplace, with a mix of Baby Boomers, Gen X, and Gen Y, this can be a great way to foster a shared understanding of generational differences in work and life expectations. Lee cautioned against "putting the cart before the horse though," and explained "before committing to creating a program, first make sure there is demand among your peers (there usually is), and second, that there is a willingness from management and HR to participate and help facilitate." If all stakeholders aren't interested, it won't sustain. He said, "The best mentor/mentee relationships are the ones that happen organically, usually because there is interest from both parties. Before creating a structured program, make sure enough interest exists on all sides."

• **WHAT IF YOUR MENTOR LEAVES THE COMPANY?** With the average duration of a job being about three years and the fact that most people change jobs eleven times throughout their lives, chances are your mentor might leave. Lee actually doesn't think that's a problem. He says, "For a young person, in some ways, that's the best scenario. Now you have someone that will be in a similar or more senior position at another company. Now you have a contact at another company and they can offer perspective outside of your company." Lee says to make sure you maintain the relationship but then also find a replacement mentor at your own company. He says, "This gives you an excuse to have two great mentors!"

• **PAY IT FORWARD.** Later in your career, remember how you got started. Did someone mentor you? Guide you? Help you navigate sticky situations? Make sure that you pay it forward and go be a mentor to someone else. Help other young workers as much as you can. You owe it to yourself and the world.

Dating in the Workplace

At my first job there was this guy—let's call him . . . Marcus. Marcus and I started chatting at an assistant's birthday party one night by the bar. Marcus was attractive and had been an assistant at the company for a year or so longer than me. Marcus and I had a connection of some sort—or at least I thought we did. Marcus e-mailed me at work and asked if I wanted to "do drinks" one night and asked about my availability. Remember, it's cool to be busy so everyone kept a schedule and calendar for themselves. I was available. We scheduled a time that week to grab drinks and he told me his favorite place was called Chocolat on Melrose. I'd never been there before.

We go to this restaurant/bar and sit in the corner. The place was dimly lit—very drinks/date-ish. He told me he was interested. He told me I'm the Jewish ambitious girl that his mother would approve of. Kind of forward, right? He told me he liked hearing my ideas about my future (my Intern Queen ideas) and wanted to hear more. He told me he wanted to spend more time together. He seemed nice and we talked for hours that night. This was right before the holiday break. You see, in the entertainment industry, one of the perks is that you get a holiday break—it's like you never left college. The industry as a whole basically shuts down for two weeks and the agencies close their doors—it's amazing. Marcus told me that we'd stay in touch over the holiday and we did. I was home in Clearwater, Florida, and we exchanged several text messages.

At the beginning of our break, we spoke all of the time via text, but as the two weeks went on, we spoke less and less. When we got back to Los Angeles, I thought the two of us would spend time together but when I brought it up to him over our assistant instant messenger system he said he'd "check his avails and get back to me." Uh oh. Not the best response from the person who wanted to introduce me to his mother after our first drinks date. Weeks went by and still no date number two. Hmm . . . Then I remembered overhearing some other girls in the office talking about having drinks with Marcus at Chocolat. It turns out that was his "place"—apparently that's where he took all of the girls for drinks and probably confused them all as much as he confused me. I don't think I ever spoke to Marcus again—seriously. Be careful. Reputations stick and we live in a small world. I continue to cross paths with Marcus every so often.

The tough part of this conversation is that some people date their coworkers all the time. And sometimes it works! When you hear stories like that it's hard to tell people not to date their coworkers. So my advice is going to fall somewhere in between. If you really like a coworker and think there might be potential, go on a date but keep it classy and try to take it slow. You don't want to complicate your relationship more than you have to. And you know what? Maybe it will work out. But just be prepared for it not to work out and the scenario of you having to face this person every day in whatever capacity you normally work with them. Remember, work crushes are normal—but keep them as just a crush if you can unless you really feel true feelings are developing. Regardless of the industry that you are in, it's a small world and you always have to imagine that the person you are hooking up with might be a future boss one day.

Relationships in the Workplace

Okay, so what about those cute married couples you meet who have been working at the same company together for years? If they hadn't been able to date each other, would they have found the happiness they have today? Here are some tips on how to handle dating, hooking up, and relationships at work.

• **KNOW YOUR COMPANY POLICY.** Make sure you know if your company has a formal policy in place about relationships in the workplace. You don't want someone else pointing it out to you.

• **STAY AWAY FROM FLIRTATIONSHIPS.** My friend Rob (the writer) made up the word *flirtationship*. If you have real feelings that you need to explore with someone at work, explore them. You don't need to be known as the company flirt.

• **RECOGNIZE SEXUAL HARASSMENT.** Make sure if a relationship is forming, it's mutual. If you ever feel uncomfortable with the way someone is interacting with you in the workplace, bring someone else into the conversation (the best place to start is usually with your HR department).

• **YOU'RE NOT IN HIGH SCHOOL.** If you are involved in a relationship with a coworker, respect the workspace and the professionalism. No making out, holding hands, or canoodling at work.

• **STAY AWAY FROM THE INTERNS.** It's never appropriate to flirt with, hit on, or have any sort of romantic activity with an intern. Wherever there is an intern, there is a parent close behind. And often, you'll be in charge of giving them assignments so it could be viewed as an abuse of power.

• **KNOW HOW TO HANDLE A BREAKUP.** It may sound morbid but what are you going to do if it doesn't work out? And you still have to see them in the office every day? Have some sort of plan in mind and ask yourself before getting into a relationship at work if it will have been worth it should the relationship fail.

• **WHAT TO DO WHEN YOU HATE PEOPLE YOU WORK WITH** A close friend of mine, Abby, has a girl who absolutely hates her and goes out of her way to talk smack about her to other people in her industry. They worked together at my friend's former company and this girl actually took over her old role. My friend has gone out of her way to fix the relationship, help her, train her, help her friends, but this girl is still willing to gossip about her nonstop. Instead of confronting her, my friend has decided this battle isn't worth fighting. Confronting this situation might just lead to more gossip and more negative words.

Sometimes you just nod your head and tell yourself that you cannot change people. Your job isn't to create waves in the office. If it needs to be directly dealt with, go to people outside of the situation for advice and bring the least amount of people into the situation. Remember, you didn't pick these people. They are probably going to be working with you for a while. This is your work life, not your personal life, so you don't have to be best friends with the person. Just do your best to hold your head high and stay above it all.

What If You Were Hired When Others Were Fired

In talking to many of my former Intern Queen ambassadors, one common question was, how do you act when you know that coworkers are sour toward you because you were hired when their former coworkers have recently been let go? The situation can feel overwhelming and the responsibilities and expectations can feel increasingly large. I spoke to Cat Pylant, who works at WilsonHCG, a recruiting firm. She says, "You have to take on everything that comes at you. You might even end up doing tasks that don't fall under your job description. Have the 'whatever it takes to get the job done' mentality." And Cat's right. You have to do whatever you can to get through that time. It might be uncomfortable, you might question why you were hired and others were let go, but they were most likely for reasons that have nothing to do with you personally. What you'll find is that this is a big opportunity for you to prove yourself to your hiring manager and to your coworkers. Don't worry so much about winning them over; focus on performing well and putting out great quality work and you'll be surprised how quickly an uncomfortable situation can turn into an okay one. Cat also brings up the importance of having uncomfortable conversations and facing them head on. In the end, she says people will respect you for it.

Networking

I'm a US Airways flyer. I'm very loyal to that airline and I'm a Gold member (almost Platinum!). One of the perks of my job as CEO of both InternQueen.com and LaurenBergerInc.com is that I travel all of the time. During the year, I'm on the road upward of one hundred days. I rack up a lot of frequent flyer miles. Typically, when I fly I get first class upgrades. And usually if you are flying with a companion and you purchased your ticket with them, they will get upgraded to first class as well.

My boyfriend, Mike, and I were both upgraded to first class on a flight from Philly to Los Angeles, which was about a six-hour trip. We were stoked to be upgraded but when we looked at our seat numbers we realized we weren't seated together. He had the window seat in row one and I had the window seat in row four. We went up to the gate attendant in Philly and asked if she could change our tickets so that we both could sit together. She said she couldn't do anything but reassured us that the people in first class were "so nice" and would definitely change seats with us. Great! We boarded the flight and Mike asked the guy next to him if he would mind trading seats with me. The man mumbled some sort of reason that he needed to be in the front-row aisle seat. Okay . . . So then I sat down in my seat, waiting for the passenger next to me to arrive. Finally, a man in his late fifties sat down next to me and greeted me. I asked if he would mind trading seats (in first class, mind you) and he said no. We couldn't believe it. We were stuck with a bunch of first-class seat snobs (but I guess, on the bright side, we *were* stuck in first class). Anyway, Mike and I growled a bit and retreated to our separate seats for the six-hour flight. About five minutes in, the passenger next to me, who refused to change seats so that my boyfriend could sit next to me, started talking to me about my business. He had a million questions! Mike looked back at the guy in disbelief that he would try to have an entire conversation with me after being such a jerk. I was polite and spoke with him. He gave me his card before he got off the plane. For him, this was definitely a networking opportunity. For me, not so much. He would always be the guy who wouldn't let me sit next to my boyfriend on the plane. All that I could think about was that first impression—that he wouldn't change seats with me! A few months later, I got an e-mail from that same airplane guy. It was from a random e-mail address (I had since thrown the card away). It said:

> *Dear Lauren,*
>
> *I hope you remember me. I'm the guy who wouldn't switch seats in first class when you and your boyfriend wanted to sit together. Hope you are well. I was thinking that maybe we could work on some projects together? Call me this week?*

Needless to say I never responded to the e-mail. I mean . . . really? Was this guy serious? That's a networking story gone badly for you. Remember, first impressions stick.

You should be networking in two ways: by building relationships inside the office and within your company; and externally, by building relationships with people outside of your company

Networking Internally

Networking happens day in and day out. There is a preconceived notion that you have to be at a networking event to network when, in fact, you are networking every day—whether or not you know it. Every time you meet another person and take the time to get their name and potentially exchange information, you are networking.

The word *networking* has a bad connotation but it really just means connecting genuinely with another person. A former intern of mine, Lauren Mitchell, who now works for the Atlanta Dream (the WNBA team) says that she's been able to successfully network within her company by showing interest in the overall business and not just the department she works within. Another one of my former ambassadors, Joanna Mackow, who works in human resources at BASF Global—The Chemical Company, says, "To network within my company I've joined several different affinity groups (women in business, young professionals, African Americans in business, etc.). One common misunderstanding people have is that you can only join the group if you fall into the target audience, this is most definitely not the case."

• **BE AWARE OF WHAT THE PEOPLE HIGHER UP ARE DOING.** What are they proud of? What are they working on? You can't just stay pigeonholed inside of your own bubble. Make sure you are complimentary and always supportive. Stay on top of other people's accomplishments. Support their work. One of my secret tricks is to set Google Alerts so that every time my former boss is mentioned in the media I get a Google Alert right to my inbox with the link. If the article is means for a congratulations or celebration, I'll forward it to my former boss and say congratulations!

• **KEEP PERSONAL STATIONERY IN THE OFFICE.** Whenever someone does something really nice for you or helps you out at work in a big way, send them a personal note. It will go a long way. Additionally, anytime it's someone's birthday, make sure to send them a note—I promise this is a personal touch that will go a long way. Keep a calendar with everyone's birthdays in it.

• **NETWORK WITH THE HIGHER-UPS.** If you can't get to them, get to their assistants. Never underestimate the importance of a powerful executive's assistant. In fact, we are so frequently taught to network with the higher-ups but oftentimes it's the assistant who influences their boss's decisions, knows who's getting hired and who's getting fired, and is extremely well connected.

• **SET INFORMATIONAL INTERVIEWS WITH PEOPLE YOU ADMIRE IN YOUR COMPANY.** E-mail executives whom you've formed relationships with and ask if they'd be willing to sit down with you for fifteen minutes to hear how they got started and give advice. You will find that a large percentage of people are willing to pay it forward and help people when they're first starting out within an industry.

• **ATTEND COMPANYWIDE EVENTS AND GO OUT OF YOUR WAY TO TALK WITH NEW PEOPLE.** You need to be seen and recognized within the company. If two executives are in a meeting and your name comes up, you want them to have an idea of who you are. Get involved with any company activities (baseball teams, book clubs) and try to attend as many company-related happy hours as you can. These are important events for you to be seen. Even if you feel like you are locking yourself in the office and not coming up for air. Sometimes you just have to be thoughtful of the events that matter. You have to be particular in selecting your meetings and lunches. You never know where you are going to run into people. It's always good to run into "people you know" in different places.

• **SAY HELLO TO SUPERIORS.** Now, I'm not telling you to be annoying. I'm telling you to be polite and courteous while remembering your role. When you are passing an executive that you've been introduced to, don't be afraid to say hello, and mention their name. "Hello, Steve!" Or "Hello, Mrs. Rabbenstein." If you are wondering whether to use first name or last name, just go with whatever they were introduced to you as. You want them to know who you are and remember you. They might ignore you, they might treat you as an assistant, but you know what? You can say hello to them.

• **STAY ACTIVE ON COMPANY SOCIAL PLATFORMS.** Cat Pylant from WilsonHCG says, "It's really important to be outgoing and keep really high communications inside the company. At my company, we have an internal Facebook page that I'm very active on. I'm very active on each platform that we are active on as a company so that I'm very visual to all of my colleagues. I'm proactive in setting meetings with our managers and with the CEO. I let them know I want to grow with the company."

• **TRAVELING ON YOUR PERSONAL TIME?** In a location where you could take meetings or meet workers from other company offices? Take the opportunity! Building these relationships and knowing the people that others don't know will put you ahead of the competition and help you stand out.

• **HAVE A "SAY YES" ATTITUDE.** One of my former ambassadors, Kellie, who now works for Ogilvy & Mather in Chicago, says, "I never turn down an opportunity to meet new people or learn new things. I say yes when it feels uncomfortable. I push my boundaries. I challenge myself to grow personally and professionally every day." I spend a lot of this book telling you to watch your time and say no to things. Ironically, I'm going to take a moment here to talk about when it's appropriate to say yes. If someone that you are in the process of building a relationship with asks you to do something, try to say yes. You never know who you will meet or the opportunities that might present themselves down the road as a result of you attending these functions.

• **VOLUNTEER FOR COMPANY PHILANTHROPIC INITIATIVES.** At the talent agency, they would send out e-mails every few months trying to get a group of agents together for yearly philanthropy trips. I never went on any of these trips but some coworkers of mine did. And it was one of the best professional choices they ever made. First of all, it's always good to participate in philanthropic organizations—regardless of the payoff. Second of all, my friends that went on these trips traveled with several high-level agents who also went on these trips. They spent days and nights with top executives at the company and because of that they left the trip having bonded with several of the higher-ups. They left the mission feeling great about themselves, their charitable-work contributions, and about the relationships they built and the memories they created with high-level staff.

Networking Externally

Right after I moved to Los Angeles, my friend Lauren Gold and I (both UCF alums) wanted to join the UCF alumni group in Los Angeles. We lived across the country from where we went to school and we wanted to meet some fellow Floridians. When you live so far away small communities like this are hard to find. We immediately called the UCF alumni office in Orlando, Florida, and asked how to get connected. We were told that there hadn't been a formal alumni club in Los Angeles for a few years. Guess what our next question was? You guessed it: "Can we start one?" The alumni association was ecstatic. Los Angeles was a great place for the university alumni association to have a presence. We were introduced to Todd, the man in LA who used to run the club, and before long we had established the official Los Angeles UCF Alumni Club. To this day, we are both the cochairs of the club in Los Angeles. We organize watch parties for football games, networking events, mixers, and parties. And the best part? We are constantly connected to our fellow alumni and also have the ability to act as connectors. It's an amazing organization and some very close friends have come from our association with the club.

Another great option is to look into your sorority or fraternity alumni group. Most of these national organizations have several alumni groups in multiple cities. Join up, attend events, and connect with as many different people as possible.

I know I keep hammering this into you, but you have to be vigilant about curating your personal brand awareness. Instead of thinking, "Where can I network?" think, "Where can I build relationships with other people?" Here are a few suggestions:

- college alumni events
- sorority/fraternity alumni groups
- church, temple, or other religious centers
- young professional organizations or local networking groups
- intramural teams (soccer, basketball)
- airplanes
- work events
- friends' birthday parties
- at the gym
- conferences
- volunteer to speak on panels
- have people shadow you at work

How to Prepare for Networking

Before I go anywhere, I like to think to myself, "How can I be the most prepared for this event?" If I'm going to the beach, I'm going to make sure to bring a cooler, snacks, water, sandwiches, five types of sunscreen, huge beach towels, a hat (just in case my hair gets gross), makeup (just in case we go anywhere afterward), and a hoodie (because I know it gets cold at night). Same goes for a networking opportunity. If I were going to attend a networking event tonight, I'd do and prepare the following:

- **SHINE UP.** I make sure I look clean, showered, stylish, and dressed for the job I want or the way I want people to see me. Your personal appearance gives people insight into who you are. The fashion that we wear lets us express ourselves. If I want this specific group of people to take me very seriously, I might go with black pants and a structured blazer. If it's more of a casual outing with young executives, I might go a little trendier. Perhaps I'll put on skinny jeans, a bright colored oversized top, and throw a more casual blazer on top of it. I would take the time to actually do my makeup, style my hair, and put on heels. I wouldn't wear flip-flops.

- **GO WITH A BUDDY.** Chandra from 99dresses.com says she goes to meet-ups with a buddy. "We share similar interests, work in the same field, and have a similar work ethic. It's less intimidating and can help break the ice, provided you don't stay glued to each other's sides the entire time."

- **BUSINESS CARDS.** I make sure I have a stack of twenty to thirty business cards with me.

- **NOTEPAD AND PEN.** I bring a small notepad and a pen (make sure it's not chewed up if that's one of your nervous habits).

- **PHONE CHECK.** I make sure my phone is 100 percent charged.

- **CASH.** You never know when you might need it.

- **CAR WASH.** If I know I need to valet, I get my car washed or drive through a car wash. There is nothing more embarrassing than driving up to a valet with a dirty car. If you live in a city where you can walk or take a cab or the subway . . . I'm jealous!

- **BRING THE EXTRAS.** I throw mints, gum, and a granola bar in my purse.

- **IMPORTANT STUFF.** I make sure I have my ID and a credit card.

- **SHADES.** If the event is outside during the day, I definitely bring my sunglasses. You don't want to be the person squinting.

- **BROWSE THE GUEST LIST.** I look at the event list on Evite, Eventbrite, Facebook, the flyer, or whatever platform the group is using to promote the event and I scan it beforehand to see who is going. I want to pinpoint interesting people from companies I'd like to do business with.

- **SET A GOAL.** I give myself a goal of how many new people I want to meet that night. It might be a small goal, maybe five or so, but something I can hold myself to so that I walk out of the event feeling accomplished.

If You're Generally Shy . . .

When I speak at colleges, I often get questions from students who aren't as outgoing as I am. They ask me how to get over being shy and how I deal with being nervous. I think setting goals in terms of how many people you'll go up to at a networking event is a great exercise, especially if you are shy. Earlier in the book, we talked about challenging yourself and getting comfortable being uncomfortable. Whenever I feel myself retreating and not putting myself out there, I challenge myself to just do it anyway—even though it doesn't feel like the most comfortable thing to do. Convince yourself that the worst thing that can happen is rejection—and we already learned how to deal with that. Another piece of advice I have for people who feel shy or are easily intimidated is to start conversations with people you wouldn't normally speak to. Take the sandwich artist at Subway or the person bagging your groceries at Trader Joe's. Ask them how their day is going so far. When you leave the store say goodbye and tell them to have a nice day. Challenging yourself is really the key and you will see positive habits start to develop.

Next you need a way to keep everything organized. If you are going to meet someone, what is your follow-up plan? When will you reach out? How will you store your information? What are some good strategies for staying organized?

Quick Business Card Rules

Don't be upset if you don't get your own set of business cards. It's actually very common for young people to not get their own business cards until their third or fourth job. Because of the high level of turnover for entry-level hires and the type of work they are spending their time on, most companies don't provide business cards for them. If you do have business cards, remember to have them with you at all times. I always make sure that I have a stack in my purse before I go anywhere. As I mentioned earlier, you NEVER know when you will meet someone and need to pass along your information. Even more important than giving out your information, is getting business cards from executives that you meet. Make sure to ask people for a business card and if they don't have one, ask them for the best way to stay in touch. Don't let an executive who doesn't have a business card block you from asking for a way to stay in touch. Before you give someone your business card, I suggest saying something like "I'd love to give you my business card so that we can stay in touch." Don't just throw the business card in their face. Also, have an organizational system for business cards. I would suggest emptying out your bag or wallet every Monday and adding all of your new contacts into Outlook on your computer. E-mail everyone you meet ASAP to follow up. They aren't going to remember you if you wait too long to follow up. I hate keeping loose business cards around as they just create clutter and I forget who people are over time. So as soon as I get them, I enter their info into my Outlook account, make a note as to where I met them, and get rid of the card.

How to Make the Most of Your Professional Contacts

You already know my rule about staying in touch with your professional contacts three times per year. I stay in touch with my professional contacts once during the fall, once during the spring, and once during the summer. And if I can't think of anything to say, I turn to the holidays or send them an e-mail on their birthday. I also make sure to have as many of my contacts' birthdays on my work calendar as possible. My new Windows Phone actually syncs with my Facebook so that all of my Facebook friends' birthdays appear on my work calendar. This is extremely helpful.

So let's go through a simple example. You are an event planner and you attend an event-planning conference over the weekend. You met a lot of people, can't really remember exactly who was who, and have a pile of business cards lying at the bottom of your Michael Kors. Here's what should happen:

To-Do List for the Day after a Networking Event

• **REMOVE.** Take them out that night and put them on your desk or wherever you put your to-do pile for the next business day.

• **ORGANIZE.** Enter all of the contact information you received into your Microsoft Outlook or Gmail contacts.

• **E-MAIL.** That same day, take an hour to individually e-mail everyone. Your note should look something like this. Let's pretend the person you met was Phyllis:

Hi Phyllis,

Great meeting you at the event planners' conference over the weekend! I really enjoyed chatting with you and learning more about your organization. I wanted to send over my contact information so that we can connect in the future.

Best,
Lauren

Now, if you wanted something from this person (in a more immediate way) you could send something like this:

Hi Phyllis,

Great meeting you at the event planners' conference over the weekend. We have so much in common! It was great hearing about your similar experiences with clients and events. I'd love to talk more and ask you some questions about an upcoming event I'm having. Do you have some time in the coming weeks?

Best,
Lauren

• **CONNECT ON SOCIAL MEDIA.** Connect with Phyllis on LinkedIn and follow her on Twitter if you can. I think it's fine to avoid Facebook for work-related contacts. You can like her work page if she has one.

How to Follow Up with the People You Meet While Networking
Since following up with professional contacts is one of the most important parts of the book, I wanted to come up with a way for you to

remember what to do after meeting a potential contact. I have a mnemonic for this section, get excited:

RALPH CALLED TAYLOR A FLIRT

*R*alph	*R*ecognize
*C*alled	*C*onnect
*T*aylor	*T*rack
A	*A*dd value
*F*lirt	*F*ollow up

• **RECOGNIZE.** Whenever you meet someone, you have an opportunity. Make sure to recognize the potential. It's your job to recognize the opportunity and get the person's information. You never know where this opportunity might lead.

• **CONNECT.** You must do your job and connect with this person right after you meet her. But I want you to think about who else you could connect this person with that might be helpful for her. Remember, you can't connect her with someone unless you know that person will fill a need she has or you have a great relationship with her. If you have someone that you can connect another person to—to solve a problem or help her get ahead—do it. In fact, do it multiple times. Introduce one person or multiple people to other people that have similar businesses or could benefit from knowing one another. Be an introducer. If you are helping other people constantly, I promise, they will be around when you need help. Be a connector and help whenever possible.

• **TRACK.** Follow your new contact online. Set up Google Alerts so that every time their name or the name of their company is in the news, you can follow the story. If congratulations are in order—send them over! You don't need to do this for everyone you meet, but for your important contacts stay on top of what they're up to.

• **ADD VALUE.** How can you help this person? How can you add value? Is it sending them relevant articles about their industry? Is it introducing them to the right people? Is it sending them ideas?

• **FOLLOW UP.** If you don't hear back from someone after you reach out, follow up two weeks later. You can put *follow-up* in the subject of the e-mail and send a short e-mail politely following up with the contact. Again, it's your job not only to keep in touch with this person on a regular basis (three times per year) but also to keep your promises. If you told someone that you met last night who works in photography that you are going to introduce them to your friend who is looking for a photographer for a project, make the introduction. In my experience, it's rare to find people who follow up or do what they say they are going to do and you'll stand out if you are one of those people.

Networking Must-Dos

• **LOOK PEOPLE IN THE EYE.** I hate when I'm trying to have any kind of conversation with someone at a networking event and they are looking around the room. I get it. They are looking to see if anyone noteworthy or better to talk with walked in. But regardless of who I am and what I can do for them, I deserve their respect, their attention (at least for the moment), and their eye contact.

• **GET OFF YOUR PHONE.** When you are at an event you might have to exchange text messages with a friend who is meeting you there or answer a couple of work e-mails. I understand. But if you are in a corner on your phone you are basically saying, I don't want to talk with anyone. You may as well be wearing giant headphones. You are (maybe purposely) trying to give the vibe that you have more important things to do—but trust me it's not working. Additionally, if you are speaking with someone, don't start playing around with your phone. It's so rude to do that in the middle of a conversation. I'm sure whatever is happening can wait and if it can't, politely excuse yourself.

• **STOP ASKING, "WHAT DO YOU DO?"** Often people at networking events are so consumed with meeting people that work in their industry that they overlook interesting relationships that are right in front of them. Like I mentioned earlier in this section, don't be networky, be as genuine as possible—get to know people. Remember, everyone knows everyone. You never know when you'll tap into a specific contact and you never know who knows who. Great questions to ask are "Where are you from?", "Where did you go to school?", and "What brings you to this event?" Ideally, you can connect with the person about something nonwork related and build a more natural connection. Some people are terrified of these dreaded mixers. If you need to, write down some icebreaker-type questions and put them in your purse.

• **KEEP AN OPEN MIND.** The second you hear that someone doesn't work in your industry, don't walk away from them. You never know how the two of you might be of help to each other in the future. Not to mention, you never know who that person might know. Contacts are valuable— regardless of the industry they work in. Try to be open-minded when it comes to meeting people who work in fields that aren't exactly related to your own. You never know where your career path is going to end up. People change jobs all the time these days. You never know when someone will all of a sudden work in your field—or when you may work in theirs. Quick example: Years ago, I spoke at Wake Forest University. I got lost on campus and ended up asking for directions in a store that prints T-shirts for fraternities and sororities. The people were extremely helpful. I grabbed their card on the way out the door. Four years later, I decided to print some Intern Queen T-shirts. I had no idea where to start. I was digging through my contacts trying to see if I knew anyone and I found the contact information for that T-shirt store in North Carolina. I called them (really just to get advice) and I ended up printing my first run of shirts with them. Two years later, I'm still working with them. You never know when you'll utilize a contact.

• **LISTEN FOR PROBLEMS.** When you are at networking events you want to listen for problems so that you can offer solutions. For example, say you are overhearing a conversation about how someone is looking for a great restaurant to take their parents to in Los Angeles next weekend. You know everything there is to know about restaurants in LA. You approach them and say you couldn't help but overhear their issue with the restaurants and that you know of some great locations. You name a few and then offer to e-mail them a list of your favorites and where you've taken your parents before. They give you their card. Connection made! (Now, don't forget to follow up!) Remember, **R**alph **C**alled **T**aylor **A** **F**lirt. **R**ecognize, **C**onnect, **T**rack, **A**dd value, **F**ollow up.

Phew! I know that was a lot of information, but it's necessary. Relationships are probably the most important part of the workplace. Since we covered so much ground, I want to provide a quick checklist so that you can make sure you read through all of the different sections. To do a quick recap, the chapter covered

- navigating office politics (POP)
- relationships with your boss
- relationships with your coworkers
- how to find a mentor
- rules for dating in the workplace
- how to work with people you dislike
- how to network
- where to network
- how to network internally (within your company)
- how to network externally (outside of your company)
- must-haves for networking

- must-dos for networking
- staying in touch with professional contacts

I'm confident at this point that you are going to be able to make the most of every relationship-building opportunity inside and outside of your current job. Remember, you never know who you'll meet and what part they'll play in your life. It only takes one person to change the course of the rest of your career.

CHAPTER 6

Oops, I Did It Again

You messed up. We've all been there. As you know from reading this book so far, I've definitely been there. Every day, I get a slew of e-mails from all kinds of people asking me how they can fix slip-ups in the office or how they can navigate sticky situations. How do you ask for a raise? How do you stop a bad rumor? How do you repair a bridge you've burned? Can you repair it? How can you salvage a relationship with someone whose project you messed up? How can you come back from missing an important deadline at work?

The truth is, we've all messed up. Even some of my friends who are perfectionists, who pride themselves on never letting anything slip through the cracks, mess up sometimes. Problems at work happen—such is life. We are all going to make mistakes and have issues to deal with at work at one time or another. Just like anything else in life, it's all about how we deal with them, how we learn from them, and how we fix the problem when it comes around a second time (as it always does).

In this chapter, I'm going to explore some of the most common issues in the workplace: What to do when you burn a bridge with a professional contact, how to handle missing a deadline, telling your boss you can't take on any more work, sending your boss to the wrong event, how to handle feeling stuck at your job, speaking about a work issue in front of the wrong person, how to handle a moody boss and coworkers who gossip, hookups at work, and how to manage raises and promotions that seem unfair at work.

ISSUES WITH ACTUAL WORK (THINGS THAT COME ACROSS YOUR DESK)

COMMON PROBLEM: You burned a bridge with a professional contact.

EXAMPLE: You are a publicist. You are representing the Cat Whisperer (pretty cool!). You pitch a story idea to *Favorite Pets* magazine. You e-mail them and explain why an interview with your client the Cat Whisperer would be a great idea for the magazine. They write you back and tell you they're not interested. You write back asking why, and that you'd love to learn more about what they are looking for so that in the future you can cater your pitches accordingly. They don't enjoy your persistence and ambition. They write you back a nasty letter that says, "We know our readers better than you. Please don't pitch us again. We don't appreciate your attitude." You feel like you burned a bridge with a major magazine editor in the animal space. You read your e-mail again and determine that maybe it could have been read in the wrong way and seen as aggressive. You make a note to tweak your e-mails in the future and read them back to yourself before sending. We all make mistakes, it's just a matter of figuring out how to fix them so they never happen again.

HOW TO FIX: First, I suggest apologizing. Send them an e-mail. Something like this, "I'm so sorry if I offended you in any way. I really enjoy your magazine and hope we can work together in the future. Please let me know if I can ever be of help to you." We all mess up. But we don't all take responsibility for our actions. Once we realize we mess up there are certain things we can do to fix the situation. Once we do those things and put our checks in our boxes (as I mentioned in chapter one), it's time to move on.

Even though it feels uncomfortable, mention the issue to one of your superiors. You don't want them to find out from someone that's not on their team. What if they are in a meeting with this magazine and the editor mentions your issue? It's your job to keep them in the loop. And who knows? They might even be able to fix the problem if they know the person and have a proven track record with them. With higher-level executives come more years of experience, so usually the higher-ups can apologize on your behalf and help with these problems.

COMMON PROBLEM: You didn't complete a project on time. Not only is your boss upset but now a client is upset as well. What do you do?

EXAMPLE: You were working on a story for *Seventeen* magazine on internships and your deadline was Friday. You got really busy on Friday afternoon and forgot to hand in the story. It was supposed to go live on Monday morning. Now it's Monday morning and your boss wants to see you.

HOW TO FIX: First, take responsibility for what happened. Explain that you understand the bigger picture. Don't blame others or come up with a ton of excuses. It's a lot less painful to just take responsibility and admit your mistake and people will respect you for it.

In this case, you would obviously go write the article. If you are in a situation where there isn't a quick fix, ask your supervisor what you can do to fix it. Don't make the supervisor feel like they need to clean up your mess. Demonstrate that you can go above and beyond to rectify the situation. This way, your supervisor sees you taking responsibility and will have some faith that you won't do it again.

Continue to go above and beyond and make your supervisor feel like you are learning from what happened. Adopt a new system, get ultra-organized and on top of things, and show you are never going to let that happen again.

We spoke about things slipping through the cracks in earlier chapters. We need to nip this problem in the bud right away. I spend so much time in this book talking about the importance of meeting deadlines and properly managing your time and we need to find a strategy that works for you. Think about ways to fix the problem in the future. If you really don't know how to fix this issue, discuss strategies with coworkers or other people who have similar jobs; they might have an organizational system that makes sense for you. The reason your boss is upset is because you've just made them look bad to their boss. And who knows, maybe their boss is getting heat, too. The chain of command at corporations goes up pretty high, and you never know who your mistake might be affecting. What if your assignment was sponsored by a company paying for that space? If you miss deadlines with clients involved the client could ultimately pull out of the deal, meaning your company would lose money. My point here isn't to scare you, it's to make you think twice as hard about missing deadlines and understand that there might be a lot riding on that one little assignment of yours.

COMMON PROBLEM: Your boss is asking you to take on too many projects and clients. What do you do?

EXAMPLE: You run the marketing department for a chain of popular burger joints in the South. Your responsibilities include overseeing all of the private events in your region, publicity for the region, making frequent store visits, and building relationships with all of the large vendors in the area. Your days are packed; you oversee five in-store marketing representatives and can barely come up for air. You are always looking for ways to lessen your workload so that you can have a life. Your boss calls and tells you he has another assignment for you. He wants to add three more locations for you to oversee. He tells you to consider it a compliment. You ask if that means you are going to lessen your workload in terms of your current projects and tasks, and he says no. You have a problem. You are mentally and physically at capacity. If you brought on another client or project, the rest of your work would severely suffer. You would normally jump at an opportunity but this is no longer something you can manage. What do you do?

HOW TO FIX: First, make sure you understand exactly what your boss is asking you to do. Request a short meeting with him or her to explain your workload. Make sure you use a very sincere tone of voice so it doesn't come across like you are whining.

Explain that you take pride in your work and want to make sure that you are able to give one hundred percent to any project you take on. Tell your boss that unfortunately, you don't think it's possible to handle any more projects at this time without removing some of the current responsibility. In most situations, your boss might be bummed, but will understand and appreciate your honesty. It's better for your boss to find out this way instead of by you not executing to the best of your ability. There comes a time when you have to protect yourself, your personal life, and the quality of your work.

Another option here is to use the advice card. Explain what you are experiencing to your boss and ask what they suggest you do in this situation. Let them give you the answers.

COMMON PROBLEM: Your boss is going to a meeting and you gave her the wrong address. What do you do?

EXAMPLE: My friend Sara is a teacher. Sara set up a parent-teacher conference for herself, the school principal, and the parents of a problem child at school. The meeting is initially scheduled for Monday at 3:30 P.M., immediately after school. The day of the meeting, the parent texts Sara and asks if he can move the meeting to Tuesday. Sara texts back yes and makes a mental reminder to e-mail her principal. Sara sees her principal in the hallway and tells her the meeting has been changed to Tuesday. She tells her she'll e-mail over the meeting information. Sara forgets to send the e-mail. The day of the meeting arrives and Sara and the parent are sitting together waiting for the principal. The parent tells Sara he wants to pull his child out of the school because the principal clearly doesn't care about the performance of his child. Sara tries to confess and take the blame for the principal not attending but the parent isn't listening. The parent calls the principal and yells at her. Then, the principal calls Sara and yells at her for not telling her about the meeting. The parent almost pulled the child out of the school. Ugh. What do you do?

HOW TO FIX: In this case, you can reach out to the parent, take the blame again, and reschedule the meeting. Send the correct and updated meeting information out ASAP. After that, it's time to start apologizing. Apologize on the phone, in person, and follow up in person. Try never to do it again. Double-check your work in the future. Correct the situation immediately after it happens. Look ahead at the calendar for the rest of the week. Every single parent-teacher conference you've booked for your principal in this week must look perfect!

COMMON PROBLEM: You didn't know your room and you spoke about something in front of the wrong person. What do you do?

EXAMPLE: You work for *Entrepreneur* magazine. You are the assistant to the editor of the magazine. Your job is to always be a step ahead of her and constantly predict her next move. You are also in charge of taking notes at meetings. You are in a meeting with the entire IT team from *Entrepreneur.* Your boss is holding court and you are taking notes, per usual. She starts talking about the current outside firm that they use to market their magazine to the United States. She looks at you to make sure you are taking notes. You say to her, "I've got it all. Should I add in here that we might not work with them anymore?" You knew this from another meeting you were in. Your boss gives you *the look.* "I'm not sure what you are talking about. We'll discuss later." Uh oh. What did you do? You thought she'd appreciate your knowledge and input. She pulls you aside after the meeting and says the head of the IT department is best friends with the head of the marketing company they are about to fire and she didn't want the IT person to know. "Know your room!" she screams at you. Yikes. What do you do?

HOW TO FIX: All that you can really do here is be more observant in the future. Think before you speak and ask yourself, "Is this conversation appropriate to have in front of these people?" In our networking chapter I wrote about office politics and I suggested you be aware of relationships—who is friends with who, who is doing who a favor, and why. If you were aware of the major relationships, you would have known this.

Whenever you are hesitant about anything, about who can hear what, or what information should be shared with which people, just ask your boss or a colleague after the fact. You don't want to risk sharing the wrong information with the wrong people. As your boss told you, know your room.

ISSUES WITH YOUR BOSS OR COWORKERS

COMMON PROBLEM: Your boss just screamed at you in front of other people. He or she made you feel really stupid. You want to scream and walk out. What do you do?

EXAMPLE: You work at an ad agency. You are a junior account manager. You were helping a boss with a project and she doesn't like the progress you've made so far. She is also moody. She screams at you in front of everyone, storms back to her office, and slams the door.

HOW TO FIX: Don't scream back. I keep talking about consistency throughout the book and you need to show your supervisor that no matter what happens, you will keep an even keel. If you are going to be known as reliable, you must be predictable in terms of both actions and attitude. If your boss screams at you once, let it go. However, if it happens a few times, I suggest setting up a time to discuss the issue with your boss. Here's what to say and how to handle this conversation:

- You always want to balance a negative comment with a positive one. Mention how much you enjoy your job before raising a complaint.
- Use the advice card. "What would you do in my situation?" "How do you suggest I make things better?"
- Take the collaborative approach. "How can I become better at this task and not irritate you along the way?" "What can I do to better understand this process?" "I want to make you feel good about my progress. I want you to enjoy working with me. What are some techniques I can practice to make sure I'm constantly improving?"
- Remember, cooler heads prevail. Clear eyes, full hearts, can't lose! (Thank you, *Friday Night Lights!*)

COMMON PROBLEM: People are spreading rumors about you at work. You are scared this will harm your professional reputation. What do you do?

EXAMPLE: A coworker overheard your conversation with a client who you have a great relationship with. She thought you were being extra flirtatious with the client. You feel like your behavior was perfectly appropriate. You've worked with the client for a few months and get along well. You are constantly asking about his wife and family, and you are definitely *not* trying to sleep with him. Your coworker starts spreading rumors that you sleep with your clients.

HOW TO FIX: First of all, when other people take time out of their busy lives to talk about you in a negative way, they are usually jealous. We've all been there at some point or another. You already know that you can't control other people. Your coworkers have the freedom of speech to say whatever they want, whenever they want. Rest assured that people usually don't trust a gossip. If they talk poorly about one person, they are likely to talk poorly about another. In terms of advice for how to confront this situation, I suggest the following steps:

First, identify what people are saying about you. Take a moment to decide if it's something worth worrying about or if it's something you should laugh at and brush off (tap into your confidence here). If there's truth to the rumor, take it as constructive criticism and work to make sure your conversations are more professional.

If there's no truth to it, continue to do what you are doing, and continue to be great at it. If you know that your boss would be happy to hear about the great relationship you've established with the client, you are doing nothing wrong. However, if you think your boss might question your phone antics with the client, it might be time to change your ways. Once you decide if you want to validate their concern, make a decision and stick to it. Ignore the gossip.

COMMON PROBLEM: You got drunk with your coworker and kissed him. What do you do?

EXAMPLE: Jerry from legal is a giant flirt. He is one of the only men in the office. He is constantly giving you *the look*. He's a gorgeous man. You know it—so does everyone else. Last night at happy hour things got a little hot and heavy. Awkward! What do you do the next day?

HOW TO QUICK FIX: At this point in your life, you should know a hookup when you see one. If this was a hookup and nothing more—joke about it, mention it should stay on the "DL," and move on with your life. Try not to let it happen again. If you really have feelings for the person, follow my dating your coworkers rules in the previous chapter. Definitely don't be aggressive, overbearing, or obsessively post things on his Facebook wall.

ISSUES WITH PAY/PROMOTIONS

COMMON PROBLEM: You are unhappy in your job. You've been miserable for weeks and everyone around you knows it. You're starting to feel stuck—the dreaded "stuck" feeling in the work-place. What do you do?

EXAMPLE: I can use my own example here. I felt extremely "stuck" at the talent agency as I put my time in working for two different agents from 2006–2008. I felt like I was going nowhere at that job. No one respected me, no one thought I was good at my job. No one wanted to promote me, and I wasn't getting a raise anytime soon. I didn't know what to do. I knew I couldn't just leave without snagging a new job first and having steady income coming in. My parents didn't get it. They thought I was crazy to leave that "glamorous job." I got to a point where I was very low and hated going into work. I'd get anxiety and cry on my way in. I felt like a prisoner trapped at my job. Here's what I did to get unstuck.

HOW TO QUICK FIX: Unfortunately, there isn't really a quick fix here. I'll share the process that I followed and the process I instruct my network to follow when they determine it's time to leave a job.

The first step is to make sure you are a hundred percent certain about your decision. There is a difference between really wanting to leave your job and running away from something because a challenge presents itself. There is no job that will always be smooth sailing. In my case, when things get rough, I get jealous of the baristas at Starbucks. They do their jobs and go home and don't have to think about work until the next day. But of course there is some drama and hardship in their jobs as well—some sort of power politics, attitudes, or work challenges. It's just that the grass always seems greener. Make sure you are leaving for the right reasons. If you are brutally unhappy, don't want to get out of bed in the morning, and cry on your way to work—those are some signs that it might be time to leave. (Yes, I've been there.) If you are debating a potential departure, don't tell the people that you work with. You can talk to your close friends and family about your wanting to leave your job but don't start telling your professional contacts until you want your boss and coworkers to know. You also don't want to leave until you find a new position. Of course, if they find out you are trying to leave they might let you go. If your boss finds out you are looking, I suggest telling them the truth. Tell them in the most polite way possible that you were just looking around to see what's out there. If you don't have any offers on the table, you don't want to be too in depth as you don't want this plan to backfire against you. If you know your boss is going to find out you are looking from someone else, try to get to your boss before others do. Regardless of the situation, people like to be kept in the loop. Tell your boss what's going on as she won't enjoy hearing about her employee from anyone that's not you. It will make her look like she doesn't have control of her team and office.

If you enjoy your position but dislike your company, it's time to look around at other options. Research companies that are similar to yours, look up the executives, and see what connections you have in common. A friendly referral would be the best case scenario. Have a sit-down, informational meeting with the contact, and if it goes well consider applying for that company.

Don't just take another job to take another job. You are a valuable employee and you deserve to work somewhere you are passionate about. Be patient while you search for that place. Make a target list of ten to twenty companies where you'd like to work. If the decision is more position based than company based, make a list of everything you'd like that position to include. Start looking—search the job boards, see what's available. Comb through your social networks. Are you connected to anyone who works at the companies you've listed as your dream company? On LinkedIn, you can filter your contacts by position or title—use that function to see if anyone you know operates in the capacity you are looking for.

Set informational meetings. Before you go after the job for real, you want to find out what you are in for. You don't want to leave one job you hate for another. Ask people if they would meet with you for a few minutes so that you can ask them questions and get advice. More people will say yes than you think. Ask them about their responsibilities and their day to day at the company, explain what you are looking for in a role, and ask how that translates at their company. Start applying, sending résumés, and going out for interviews—informational interviews and actual interviews. And try not to tell your current boss until you have an offer.

COMMON PROBLEM: You finally muster up the courage to ask your boss for a raise. You have the conversation and they come back to you and say no. You didn't even think about them saying no. What do you do?

EXAMPLE: You're working for a start-up in Silicon Valley. It's a very cool company and definitely a job that other people want. You've been working there for more than six months and feel like it's time for a raise. You know that making close to nothing goes along with the start-up culture, but you also know that you told the company you want to grow with them. You sit down with your direct boss and politely bring up the topic and dive into a conversation. You explain your work ethic and why you deserve a raise. Your boss tells you that he'll run some numbers and get back to you. He appreciates your coming to him. You take a deep breath! That wasn't as hard as you thought it would be! You call your parents to tell them the good news. They ask if you got the raise and you say no but that you had the conversation and it went well! Your boss seemed so understanding. At the end of the week, your boss calls you into his office. He tells you that he went over the numbers with the CFO and they appreciate your hard work but unfortunately aren't able to offer you a raise. He tells you that he's open to having a second conversation in a few months. Your face turns beet red and you feel like you've just been punched in the stomach. You didn't expect him to say no. Now what are you supposed to do? Leave the company? Hang your head and retreat back to your desk?

HOW TO FIX: You took a job at a start-up. You probably started out making a rather low salary. My advice would be to give it a year. If the company still can't give you a raise when you reach your one year mark, it might be a sign that the company isn't on track to grow as quickly as they thought they would. At a larger company, you wouldn't even be able to have a conversation about a raise until the one year mark. You wouldn't be eligible for a promotion for eighteen months and the average raise would be only 3 percent. If you enjoy your work and can potentially see a future with the company, I would suggest retreating to your desk and putting in your time (some good ole hard work). Have a follow-up conversation with your boss when your one-year anniversary with the company comes around. Have a specific raise in mind and specific reasons ready on why you deserve the raise and go in asking for a little bit more than you expect so that after negotiations, you end up where you want.

COMMON PROBLEM: You find out you aren't making the same amount of money as the person in the office next to you who holds the exact same title.

EXAMPLE: You've been at the company for years. You know for a fact that the girl who just got promoted is making more than you. How do you know? Easy, she told you. You want to scream about it. You want to egg your boss's car. You feel insulted. What do you do?

HOW TO FIX: Here are a couple general points to know about salaries:

Someone's salary is usually determined by how much a company can afford to pay that person when they start at the company. Some people have agents or lawyers negotiate their job offers for them. (Note: This is something you would potentially do closer to your third job.) Some people negotiate salary bumps into their contracts, meaning that if the company wants to keep them as an employee, they need to raise their salary every year or every other year by a pre-determined amount. And unless you work in legal or human resources, you haven't seen other people's contracts.

At some companies, all entry-level employees make a certain amount, but once you get out of that first job, things can change. Oftentimes people are hired at different starting salaries because they were making a different amount of money at their previous job. For example, if you made $29,000 a year at your first job and you tell a potential employer that, they probably will not offer you lower than

$29,000 a year as a starting salary. They might. But in most cases, they will offer you the same amount or a little bit more. If another person goes to that same employer and was previously making $32,000 a year, they might get hired at a higher starting salary. These are facts that you are most likely unaware of and will never be completely in the loop about. Your responsibility is to protect your own paycheck.

First, you need to evaluate your paycheck situation. Stop comparing it to other people. Think about your own performance. Do you deserve a raise?

Most companies are only going to give you a raise once a year. Did you just get a raise? If so, you might want to save the conversation for a year from now, depending on your company's policy. If you work for a start-up or a smaller company, they might be more willing to have the conversation more than once a year. But a larger corporation might stick to their guns and only have the raise conversation once per year.

When you go in to talk about your raise, have an idea of what you want to be making. The worst thing to do is to go in and have an employer ask what you want to be making and for you to say, "I don't know" or "Let me get back to you." You knew this conversation was happening (most likely), so show your boss that this is a priority for you and that you are ultra-prepared.

Once your boss tells you what they can pay you, you can say something like "Is there any wiggle room on that or is that as much as we can do?" Once they respond, you either accept the raise (graciously) or decline and say that you appreciate the raise but unfortunately you are going to seek out other opportunities. Of course, ideally, you don't want to leave one opportunity until you find another.

In chapter one, I spoke about not taking things personally. You could be the best employee on the planet but if the company cannot find the funds to give you the raise you are looking for, they just can't. Business is business. Just because it may look like the company has a ton of money, you haven't seen their books, you haven't seen the cash flow, and you haven't seen the other expenses they are responsible for.

COMMON PROBLEM: Your friend got promoted. You didn't and you don't know when you will. What do you do?

EXAMPLE: You started your job two years ago, on the exact same day as your coworker Darla. You like Darla and you are friends with her outside the office but you don't think Darla is better at her job than you are. Darla just got promoted. You don't get it. Where is your promotion? What do you do?

HOW TO FIX: Don't be a bad sport. Congratulate your friend for her hard work and for getting the promotion. When it's your turn, you'd want the same respect.

Think about your time at the company. Is it time for you to have a chat with them about a promotion? Maybe take a week so that the conversation isn't stemming directly from the Darla situation. Remember, the conversation shouldn't be "Darla got a promotion, why didn't I?" The conversation should be "I've been here for X amount of years. I feel that I'm very good at what I do, and I'd like to talk with you about the opportunity of being promoted. I'd love to continue to work my way up at this company."

You can mention that you noticed some company promotions and you wanted to know if they were considering promoting you.

....

I HOPE BY BREAKING ISSUES down into these three categories (actual work, bosses/coworkers, and financial issues), I've covered a wide variety of hiccups that you might very well experience as you embark on the beginning of your career.

To leave you with one final thought, I want you to remember that everyone messes up at one time or another. It happens to all of us. In fact, I might be the queen of messing up. But it's in those moments—those embarrassing screwups where you think your world is coming to an end—that you learn the most. Before we end this chapter, I'd like for you to make one promise to yourself. I want you to promise that when you do mess up, you will take a moment, reflect on what went wrong, and learn as much as you can from the situation. And then give yourself a break.

CHAPTER 7

Channel Your Inner Entrepreneur

In today's working world, everyone is so fascinated by entrepreneur success stories like Mark Zuckerberg's and Richard Branson's that they forget one's ability to be entrepreneurial within a corporate environment. I wholeheartedly believe that there is a way to feel like an entrepreneur without owning your own business. Everyone has the ability to be entrepreneurial within their companies; they just don't know it yet.

Can you organize, manage, and assume the risk of a project or concept within your current company structure and still feel entrepreneurial? Yes, you absolutely can. I would go further and say that in order to succeed within your role you need to be entrepreneurial. You need to find business, create opportunities, own your projects, and prove to your boss that you have some sense of autonomy within your position and can think on your feet. People often think, "I don't own my business. I work for someone. How can I be an entrepreneur?" But there is another way to think about it. In many ways, an entrepreneur manages his or her own time. An entrepreneur comes up with an idea, builds out the concept, and executes the plan. Now, this idea could be a tangible product, but it could also be a service, a new idea within an existing company, a project, a philanthropic activity—anything! An entrepreneur looks for ways they can add value and be responsible for their own time.

Once you demonstrate that you are capable of executing projects on your own, you might get that promotion you've been waiting for. I have a rock star example of someone who worked at a corporate company but was able to find a way to be entrepreneurial within his role. Jared Snyder works at HSBC Bank in New York City. He has worked in the banking industry since he graduated from Georgetown. About five years ago, Jared connected his hobby (playing tennis) with a niche need inside of his company. He came up with the idea of organizing unique, high-profile tennis events for the clients of the bank, where they would get to play alongside some of the best players in the world. Jared was always an exceptional tennis player, had great connections within the tennis world, and knew that his clients (wealthy executives) enjoyed tennis. I spoke with Jared and had him break down how he went from idea conception to final execution. Here are some thoughts he shared about how he brought his concept to life within a large corporation:

Jared's job was to get in front of the wealthiest, smartest, most influential people on Wall Street and build relationships with them so that he was the first phone call they made when making any banking or investing decisions. He wanted to add value to the client. The only way to differentiate was to develop relationships, internally and externally. Jared knew that he wanted to find his own niche within his company.

In 2008 and 2009, the bank started taking their top clients to the US Open, something Jared thought was sort of ho-hum. Being a tennis player, Jared thought, "How can I take something kind of average that my company is already doing and make it a unique experience the clients will never forget? How can I bring this to the next level?"

Jared decided that instead of taking clients to the US Open, he could put on an event and bring the US Open to them, giving them a "money can't buy this" type of experience.

To bring his idea to life, Jared had to create allies in the office.

He needed people to support him and his idea. In terms of building strong relationships with clients, an event like this would surely do it. So he took himself out of the equation. He thought solely about his boss: What would this event do for his boss? How would it make him look good? It was important that Jared understood his boss's goals so he could pitch this concept in a way that would resonate with his superiors.

Before bringing the idea to his boss, though, Jared had some prep work he needed to do. "You have to know your market, your competitors. You want to be well versed in your world. Who else is doing this? What other companies? Are there enough tennis players? Are there compliance issues? What kind of legal issues are there?"

Once he'd done the leg work, he went to his boss and explained why this event would make him and his department look good. When Jared approached his boss he only had notes with him, nothing formal. Jared said, "When I first approached my direct manager, I wanted to give him a high-level overview of my idea, one I felt strongly would enhance our brand in the marketplace and increase our distribution channels. I did not have a formal pitch book or pages of notes. It was simply a well-thought-through idea presented on a scale where multiple areas of the bank would benefit. As the idea gained traction and support, I most definitely presented a model for how it would take shape for the bank's clients. You just need enough notes so that you can talk about it. And if it's something you're passionate about, you'll be able to do that with no problem."

Sure, there was a chance of total rejection, but Jared wasn't nervous. "Ninety percent of my regular day job is rejection," he said. "Failure and rejection are irrelevant in life—you might feel badly here and there but they mean nothing."

Today, the *HSBC Summer Tennis Championship* is in its fourth year and Jared is about to take his vision global. The company he works for has expressed interest in Jared putting on his event for their branches in Dubai and China. I've met a lot of entrepreneurs in my life and a lot of people that work in major corporations, but I've never met someone who has been able to embrace entrepreneurship within a major company quite like Jared has. He truly represents an entrepreneur within a large corporation.

TIPS FOR ENTREPRENEURS WITHIN THE WORKPLACE

Here are a few secrets to becoming an entrepreneur within your current position or job:

• **DO YOUR JOB.** No ifs, ands, or buts. You can't embrace entrepreneurship until you are comfortable and excelling within your current position. You want executives to take notice of your great work, earn your trust, and then be open to hearing your ideas. If you aren't doing the job you were hired for, they might not be open to listening to your ideas. You were hired for a position. You know what that position is. You must complete your daily responsibilities efficiently and correctly before starting to take on additional projects. When I was at my first job, it was difficult to earn respect for my brilliant ideas because I was busy messing up my real job. Because I had no systems in place and had things slipping through the cracks left and right, nobody paid attention to my bigger ideas. You have to successfully accomplish the challenge in front of you (that is, your day job) before you can start to add more to your plate.

• **BE FAMILIAR WITH YOUR BOSS'S PROJECTS, PITCHES, AND CLIENTS.** If you understand your boss's goals and everything that goes along with her business you can pitch her ideas in a way she can gravitate towards as long as they're relevant and in line with her goals. For example, look at what Jared did. He made sure he understood that his boss wanted to build stronger relationships with clients. So when he pitched him the tennis idea, he knew to emphasize on how much this event could positively affect the relationship the firm, and specifically his department, had with the clients.

• **READ EVERYTHING.** A television writer friend, Aaron Weiner, told me that he gets up and reads everything he possibly can from 9 A.M. to 12 P.M. before he starts writing for the day. He reads the news, his favorite blogs, industry gossip, and more. He forwards me articles that are relevant to my industry (a great networking tool), is aware of everything going on in the world, is on top of pop-culture gossip, keeps up to date with industry news, and stays constantly inspired and inundated with fresh ideas. This helps him stay current and relevant, which is key for business and conversations.

• **SEEK AUTONOMY WITHIN YOUR ROLE.** Look for ways to be a self-starter within your current role. What projects can you run point on? Which projects can you make your own? What steps can you take to speak to your boss about the process? Sometimes autonomy is something that needs to be voiced so that your boss knows that's what you are looking for.

• **BE OPEN TO COLLABORATION WITH PEERS.** When I first started InternQueen.com, people would always tell me about the power of collaboration. I learned that if you share your ideas with like-minded people, you never know who might want to help support your cause. In 2006, I was in search of a design student who could draw my signature crown logo for my website. I told everyone about my ideas and people were excited to hear about them but no one actually wanted to help with them. Finally, Phil, a guy in my Spanish class, approached me. He was trying to be a professional web designer and needed more experience. He said he would draw my crown logo for $30 and I could use it indefinitely. He drew an amazing crown—I still use it on my site today as the main logo. And yes, I had him sign a contract on a piece of paper that I laminated and still keep. You see, the power of collaboration!

• **GET TO KNOW OTHER EXECUTIVES THAT RESPECT YOUR BOSS.** Getting friendly with other executives in the office can be tough. If your boss sees you acting too friendly with another executive they might doubt your intentions or your loyalty. You don't want that. Who are the executives in the building that your boss wouldn't be intimidated by if you formed a relationship with them? Remember, if you lose the support of your boss that could be a big problem. Once you identify some execs who wouldn't be an issue, try to find out what they are working on and looking for as well. In the relationship building chapter we discussed the importance of constantly putting yourself out there, becoming a connector, and doing favors for people as much as possible. Once you establish a relationship, you should be able to share ideas with them in the future and they could potentially be a support system for you.

• **TAKE CALLS FROM STRANGERS.** (Sounds crazy, right?) As an entry-level employee, you are usually in charge of answering the phones. If someone from outside the company (an entrepreneur, a salesperson, or anyone out of the ordinary) calls with an idea, think about it for a minute before you hang up the phone and tell them you don't accept solicitations. You never know when the next big idea is around the corner. When a person cold-calls you and pitches an idea it could mean that:

> • That person is actually doing their job. Perhaps she is supposed to call a certain amount of people in an industry each day to build relationships. At least you know this person is proactive.
> • Even though they are annoying and I don't care about their product, kudos to them for calling. Most would have been scared to cold call.

• Wow. That person is going after what she wants.

• Talk about chutzpah! I'm not saying that you need to sit on a call with some shady salesperson for twenty minutes. But what I am saying is that when someone calls you to pitch you certain ideas, she is clearly proving herself as a go-getter, so take a second to listen. She might have the next big idea.

• **CONNECT YOUR PASSION AND SKILLS WITH YOUR JOB.** I think Jared's example explained this pointer in the best way possible. He took his passion for playing tennis and linked that up with a great idea that would allow him to be a true entrepreneur within a company. You are always going to be better at your job and more engaged in the office if you are working on something you truly care about. Your passion always prevails and shines through.

• **IF YOU FAIL, YOU TRY, TRY, AND TRY AGAIN.** You are bound to fail. We spoke about rejection and your new way of handling it in the first chapter. You will find a way to pick yourself back up and go after what you want again (trust me, I do it on the daily).

• **TELL YOUR SUPERIORS WHAT YOU ARE PASSIONATE ABOUT.** My friend John works at an architecture firm in San Diego. After putting in one year at the company he noticed something missing: a department dedicated to sustainability and the environment. He approached his boss to express his passion for green buildings, and used examples of what other people were already doing in the industry to demonstrate the potential added value to the company. His boss agreed to the proposal, and sought to develop a department dedicated to the design and construction of green buildings. As a result of his drive to implement what he was passionate about, John was able to change the way his firm approached every project. His company now implements a nationally recognized green building system known as LEED (Leadership in Energy and Environmental Design) as the baseline standard for all their work (now the standard for all new California state and federal buildings). John led his firm to complete the design and construction of forty-five LEED certified projects including the first LEED Platinum project for the military. The firm is now nationally recognized as one of the leaders in the green building industry. In chapter one, we talked about getting comfortable being uncomfortable, being able to constantly put yourself out there, and telling others what you want to do. This is a great example of someone doing just that.

Google requires employees to spend 20 percent of their time working on projects they came up with. Now, this is an example of a company that encourages entrepreneurship. LinkedIn and Apple also have their own variations of programs like this. This is definitely an established trend and I expect to see more companies encouraging this in the coming months and years. Regardless of how much your company encourages you to channel your inner entrepreneur, you must take action. Remember, this is your life, your career—and you decide how others will perceive you, the success you will have, and what this job potentially becomes.

CHAPTER 8

I'm Just Too Busy . . . Always

A friend and I were recently on a road trip to San Diego. In the car, we got into a heated debate. I claimed that Kim Kardashian had the *busiest* schedule (note: this is pre-baby) in the world. In fact, she might be the *busiest* person alive. My friend immediately disagreed. She said that Barack Obama is obviously the busiest person on the planet and Kim Kardashian had nothing on him. I asked if she watched the Kardashian show or read about them. Clearly, the president of the United States has more important things to do than Kim Kardashian. But in terms of scheduling and commitments, I thought Kimmy K could possibly take the cake. Our debate continued for the next hour. Was Kim Kardashian *busier* than the president? And what exactly does busy mean? No, I don't think sexy photo shoots hold a candle to dealing with matters of national security but it was an interesting debate. What does busy mean in today's world? There is a difference between working a lot for the sake of working a lot and spending the time you are working doing the most important tasks.

The real question here is, what does the word busy mean to our generation? I get it. You like to work. You like to be busy. You actually look forward to checking your inbox. You can't get enough e-mails. You thrive on being busy. When you aren't busy, you start to get anxious. I can relate. I am that person. But even us workaholics, let me rephrase, *especially* us workaholics, need help with work-life balance. Over the past five years, the word *busy* has taken over our lives, flooded our vocabulary, but strangely provided all of us with some sort of self-worth. Why do we feel the need to constantly be so busy?

I feel like I'm living in a busy contest. My friend is so busy she didn't eat dinner. She hasn't slept in weeks. Another is so busy he hasn't called home in a month. My colleagues are so busy they can't keep their heads above water. They feel like they can never get enough done in a day. They eat, live, and breathe work. If they are in a bad mood, it's work related. If they can't show up for an event, it's work related. We never feel like we really achieve anything because we're too busy feeling bogged down by the next big thing. How can we feel successful when we just feel so busy?

The busy disease, as I call it, is just getting worse. Most of my peers (including myself), my colleagues, and my network are guilty of incorrectly using the busy. Being too busy can actually prevent you from getting to where you want to be inside the workplace. People who feel they are constantly too busy usually demonstrate poor work-life balance, poor ability to prioritize, lack of self-confidence, and an inability to see the bigger picture and understand their true value. In this chapter, I want to explore all sides of the busy. How does it affect you? How does it affect others? But most important, what are some tips we can integrate into our lives today to help cure the busy?

And most important, what does feeling successful even mean? And how can we stop feeling so busy and start feeling successful? To discuss this idea further I reached out to Alexis Sclamberg, career expert and cofounder of Elevate Gen Y. Alexis and I sat on a panel together last year at the National Women's Conference and I remembered her speech about what it means to feel successful.

Alexis, who used to work at a fancy law firm before starting her own business, says, "I used to always see success in my head as the corner office, high heels, and fancy suits—a very powerhouse-type job. And I realized over time (when I started wearing suits/heels) that wasn't at all what success feels like to me. What I realized was I wasn't fulfilled, I wasn't happy, and what I needed to find was something that felt good to do on a daily basis. I needed to find something that was right for me." Alexis eventually found her stride as a career expert. I explained to her that I've noticed this busy trend among my peers and other Millennials. We are all too busy for our own good. We are so busy thinking about being successful that we are forgetting how to feel successful. Alexis had some great advice for young people who just felt too busy: "People forget that you actually do better work when you are feeling good—when you have enough sleep, are feeding your relationships, and taking care of yourself. If you are taking better care of yourself—you are a better worker—you produce higher quality. You don't need to be validated by that 'work, work, work' attitude. Life is now—not just in the future. This is your life. This present moment. Give yourself permission to leave and go out to dinner with friends. This is all you've got." I'm able to relate exactly to what Alexis is saying here. We always tell ourselves that we are working hard today for tomorrow. But what about enjoying today? As Alexis said, right now all we have is today. Or to steal a line from *Rent*, "No day, but today!"

Where did this concept of "busy" start? I spoke with a recent college grad from the University of Maryland and she said the pressure starts in college. She told me that it was always a busy contest between her and her sorority sisters. Who stayed up the latest studying? Who hadn't slept in days? Who hadn't slept in weeks? She laughed recalling how irritating it got. Maybe it starts even earlier. I hear about my younger cousins who are in junior high or middle school. One of them is going pre-med! I mean, these pre-teens sound busier than I am! When does the busy feeling start and when does it stop?

When you feel busy you often work later hours, feel overwhelmed, you stress out more, and feel off center. When I feel busy, I feel like my work is in control of me instead of me being in control of my work—it's a feeling I hate. I like feeling on top of my business and my workload—I don't like when my business feels on top of me.

As I mentioned, sometimes I get jealous of my barista at Starbucks. And no—this isn't a dig at Starbucks. I'm a huge believer in Howard Schultz (Starbucks CEO) and the Starbucks way. But sometimes I get jealous of my barista because at the end of his shift, he gets to put away his equipment, clean up, and go home. He doesn't have to worry about work until his next scheduled shift. I don't have this luxury. I'm an entrepreneur and my clock never *really* stops. And I know most of you can understand. You don't have to be an entrepreneur to understand the feeling of work that just doesn't stop coming.

Now, let's talk about how to get a handle on the busy. My goal is to convince you (by the end of the chapter) that busier doesn't mean better and that working in large quantities doesn't necessarily affect the quality of your results. It is possible to work efficiently and not have to talk about how busy you are all the time. I'm going to convince you to start your day a bit earlier; spend your work time wisely; manage the expectations of your boss, clients, and coworkers; learn to say no to things; limit office distractions; and teach you how to get the heck out of the office and go enjoy your personal time. My goal is to make you understand the importance of having a life, demanding balance, and getting out of the office at a decent hour. Let's do this.

REVERSING OUR MIND-SET: QUANTITY DOESN'T EQUAL RESULTS

Dear Annoying Person at Work:

Just because you find it necessary to stay in the office until 1 a.m. every night and then brag about it the next morning to everyone else, does not make you a better worker than I am. Just because you say you live in the office, don't have a personal life, and haven't eaten in weeks, because you are so busy doesn't mean you are better at your job or a more effective worker than I am. In fact, I'm downright worried about you.

Love,
Not as busy as you but still a valid and credible person

The American Psychological Association did an interesting study back in the nineties that examined the habits of a violin player. They determined that a violin player who practices for more hours isn't necessarily better than someone who practices for fewer hours. The person who does a better job playing the violin is the one who holds more deliberate practice sessions. Now, how can we apply this to the workplace? It would seem that the person who is better at their job isn't necessarily the one spending more time in the office, it's the person getting more out of their time in the office.

We work overtime. We work long hours. We're expected to work long hours. Heck, we've started to enjoy working long hours. Lonely? There is nothing that fills the void better than diving into your workload and convincing yourself that you are the busiest person on the planet and that other people just don't understand. If you have one person who puts in ten hours a day and another who puts in seven hours a day—the person working ten hours is always the better worker and produces better, higher quality work. True or false?

False. In fact, people who tend to work more hours tend to waste more time at work. Since they are so resigned to being stuck in their workspace they tend to spend more time sitting in the office, being on the phone with others, surfing the net, or hanging out on Facebook. They have convinced themselves that any time spent in the office is purely work time, and usually this is not the case.

We need to convince ourselves that while late nights in the office happen, they don't need to be our work standard. We set the standard. We manage expectations—no one else can control this or do it for us.

TIME MANAGEMENT

I'm sitting in my home office (my desk in a corner) writing this, and I'm staring at the two books that have been sitting on my desk for about two years. One is by Regina Leeds, *One Year to an Organized Work Life*, and another is by Laura Vanderkam, *168 Hours: You Have More Time Than You Think*. Both are books that I'm fascinated by and enjoy reading over and over again. In fact, I don't think I'll ever get tired of reading about time, schedules, and setting goals. In my mind, having the perfect schedule sounds like euphoria—a fantasy land.

One time, I even hired a time-management coach! Seriously! I mentioned her earlier, Elizabeth Saunders, CEO of ReallifeE.com and author of *The 3 Secrets to Effective Time Investment*.

Back when it was a mess, I was obsessed with the idea of getting someone to organize my work life. Once I committed to changing it, it actually did wonders for myself and for my business. It's interesting how quickly someone else can approach your problem with a different set of eyes and bring solutions to the table.

Time Management Tips

• **GET UP EARLY.** I'm serious! I was never a morning person. My mother could tell you horror stories about when she would try to wake me up for school when I was growing up. I would literally scream at her (what a brat I was!). I was barely conscious but I've heard getting me up was definitely the worst job in the world. A friend of mine, Max Durovic, is the CEO of AArrow Advertising, and about two years ago we were sitting in the car together and I was complaining to him about the time difference. "We live in LA and by the time we start moving, it's already lunch in New York. By 1 P.M. our time, they are wrapping up for the day. I just can't get anything done!" Max didn't take my whining for a second. "Lauren, what are you thinking? You are an entrepreneur. You are running a business. You need to get ahead of your day, especially living in Los Angeles. You need to get ahold of your day before it gets ahold of you."

Ugh. How annoying. But he was right. I hated getting up early. I liked to sleep in until the very last second—although, conversely, I hated that feeling of being too rushed in the morning and your day starting before your eyes are open. I asked Max what he did and what time he woke up. "I'm up by 5 or 5:30 A.M. every day. I get up, check my e-mails, work out, have my smoothie, make my East Coast calls, and get ahead of everyone else." I couldn't even picture what getting up at 5 A.M. looked like. However, I had just seen a sign across the street advertising that Starbucks would start opening at 5 A.M. If Starbucks and Max were going to be awake at 5 A.M. why couldn't I?

I put this plan into action and found that getting up a few hours before my day actually needed to begin gave me more energy, helped me prepare for my day's meetings and catch up on my e-mails, and altogether feel more relaxed. I've been waking up between 5 A.M. and 7 A.M. for more than a year now and it's changed my entire work dynamic. Today, my biggest pet peeve is waking up late and having to rush right into my day. I find that having my mornings gets me a leg up on the world.

• **GET IN BEFORE EVERYONE ELSE.** I mentioned this earlier in the book. If you are physically going into an office in the mornings (which most of you are) I suggest getting in at least thirty minutes before everyone else. Use this quiet time to process the morning e-mails, get organized, and look over your calendar or your boss's schedule for the day. People aren't rushing around (yet) and you can actually get things done. Ease into your day and I promise the payoff will be worth it.

Your boss will appreciate knowing that you will be there before he or she arrives. This won't go unnoticed. The key is consistency. Try it.

• **TAKE CONTROL OF YOUR DAY BEFORE YOUR INBOX DOES.** One of the reasons many people can't leave work is because their inbox is out of control. I need to dictate how my day will run and how I will spend my time, not my inbox. When you get to your desk in the morning, I suggest trying to get at least one of your projects out of the way before spending a ton of time on your e-mails. Time-management expert Julia Morgenstern insists that you should never check your e-mail first thing in the morning. She encourages you to take ownership of your day by working on a project that's on your to-do list first instead of responding to an e-mail to help someone else cross something off their to-do list. First, look at your to-do list that you created the night before and cross at least one thing off.

• **GIVE YOURSELF A POWER HOUR.** I keep telling you to make sure you don't spend your day inside your inbox. Like I said, work on an outgoing project so that you can feel accomplished when you finally open that inbox in the morning. When you finally get to your e-mails, give yourself a power hour to run through them. Rock through all of your e-mails, file them, put your to-do list together, and make sure you are aware of everything that needs to happen that day. This isn't necessarily the time to process everything. But it's the time to organize everything on your to-do list. Make note of any tasks you might have questions about and make sure you've scheduled out enough time in your day to complete what you have in front of you. If your boss asks what you are working on or your plan of attack for the day, you will impress him or her with a schedule you've already created for yourself.

• **SELL AND PITCH DURING BUSINESS HOURS.** Time management on the job is always a struggle. You look at your to-do list, review your priorities, and most often you already have more things on your to-do list than there are hours in the day. We've all been there. I want you to really focus on selling first and updating things later. These are the activity hours. During your main business hours you should be selling and pitching your heart out. If your role is slightly more entry level and you aren't the one pitching, do anything you can to support your boss's getting her pitches and ideas out during these key business hours. Once you hit three or four o'clock you can start wrapping up, updating, organizing, following up with people, researching, et cetera. If you are located on the West Coast or outside of the United States, your selling hours might be different. I'm based in Los Angeles, so my big hours are 8 A.M. until 2 P.M. During those hours (when New York is open), I try to solely focus on generating business and being proactive. After 2 P.M., I spend time updating, organizing, researching, following up with people, and I finally get an opportunity to relax a bit. Know how to plan key activities during key times.

MANAGING EXPECTATIONS

You are instructed to set a call for your boss with a new client. You are excited to be involved in the process from the very beginning. You immediately call the client and ask to set up a call. The client also seems excited and tells you he'll send you an e-mail with his availability. He e-mails you ten minutes after you get off the phone with a question. He wants to know where your office is located. You respond immediately with a one-word answer. You say Hollywood. He responds again asking yet another one-sentence question. He wants to know if your boss likes meetings on Mondays. You are on top of your game and respond instantly with a yes. This game keeps going for about ten e-mails, back and forth. You respond almost immediately to each one. Fast forward to six o'clock. You are off the clock and it's time for you to leave. At 5:58 you see an e-mail come in again from the client. Another sentence. Ahhhh! Will it ever stop? You decide to wait until tomorrow to answer the e-mail. The next morning you have an early meeting. You go to your meeting and stroll into the office closer to noon. Your boss has an annoyed look on her face. What could be wrong? Your boss looks at you and says, "The client is upset. You had been getting back to him so quickly and now he hasn't heard from you in almost twelve hours. The client isn't happy." Your boss doesn't look happy either. "OMG." You begin to complain. Your boss cuts you off before you can say anymore. "It is YOUR job to manage the client's expectations. If the client thinks they are going to hear back from you on the hour every hour there must be a reason for it. If they think you have nothing better to do than respond to them over e-mail all day, that's what they are going to do." Your boss is right. By communicating so promptly with the client and giving short answers instead of just setting the meeting and avoiding the back and forth, you improperly managed his expectations. He expected to hear from you right away so of course he freaked out when he didn't. Lesson learned.

We spoke a little about managing others' expectations in terms of deadlines, but the most important thing to manage is the way that you communicate. In other words, how often will people hear from you? How often will you get back to e-mails? Will you answer e-mails at midnight? If you don't set boundaries and really manage people's expectations, things can go sour very quickly as this is when work really starts to consume your life.

The easiest way to help fix this is to determine when you want to work. I really believe that you get to pick the life you want. If you signed up to work weekends or later nights, so be it. But you are your own person, and, for the most part, you decide when and where people contact you. Here are a few of my rules of thumb in terms of managing others' expectations:

- Don't go back and forth with people all day over e-mail. Try to manage their expectations. They should hear from you one to two times MAX each day.

- If someone has e-mailed you multiple times with many different questions, answer them in one organized e-mail—and answer all their questions. Give them the impression that you enjoy tidy e-mails instead of getting individual mail all day. If you must, give them a call, just avoid multiple e-mails going back and forth.

Here's one more example of managing expectations. I had a book signing at Barnes & Noble recently and I knew there was a lot of pressure to get people in the door. It helped my nerves so much when I asked the manager of the store what success looked like to him. He said thirty people. I felt more confident because I was aware of his expectations and I knew I could meet them. I told my team our goal was to get sixty people in the door. Knowing his expectations were only thirty, I wanted to go above and beyond and surpass his expectations. Whenever you know someone's expectations, you can always plan more strategically and accordingly.

HOW TO EFFECTIVELY PRIORITIZE YOUR WORK LOAD AND YOUR BOSS'S WORK LOAD

Remember, you can't let your schedule control you—you have to stay on top of your workload. If you ever want to leave the office and feel okay with that decision, you must be in control at all times, manage your time well, delegate effectively, and prioritize. We discussed tips for prioritization in the last chapter. I wanted to add in a few more here that specifically relate to escaping the busy trap.

• TAKE CALLS ONLY WHEN NECESSARY OR WHEN IT MEANS FEWER E-MAILS
Calls should be scheduled for no more than fifteen minutes at a time unless you are pitching a concept and need to allow time for questions. Initial calls, sales calls, introductory calls, and favor or advice calls should take no longer than fifteen minutes. Come up with a

call-to-action plan at the end of the call and be done. For example, "Great. I'm going to send you the proposal by Monday afternoon and we'll go from there." Now, I want you to notice that I included a day here, Monday. This might not seem like a big deal but what I'm doing here is I'm setting a deadline for myself and I'm managing the client's expectations at the same time.

• **LIMIT OFFICE DISTRACTIONS.** Statistics say there is no direct correlation between longer hours worked and better hours worked. One way to make sure office hours are used productively is to limit office distractions:

> **Have a personal policy.** No calls from family or friends during the day unless it's urgent. Call them on your way to or from work or on your lunch break if you must. The hardest part of my job is that my friends think I'm always available because I run my own business. They get upset if I don't answer at 3 P.M. on a Tuesday. If you don't take yourself seriously, who will?
> **The lingering coworkers.** Look, we all like to have work friends—people we can gossip with, spend time with, and hang out with in the office. But you have to limit your "friendly" interactions. If you have a certain coworker who just pops their head inside of your office too many times each day or a coworker who plops down next to you every day and doesn't leave, start telling them that you are on a deadline. Once they see you taking your work seriously, hopefully it will ignite a fire in them to start taking their work load seriously as well.
> **Don't set meetings with distracting people.** Let's say you are working with a coworker on a project. Your coworker has a lighter workload than you do and he keeps coming around to your office to talk about your progress. This project is only one of seven things you have going on. You can't talk

about it all day—you wouldn't be able to do your job. Instead of ignoring the subject, I encourage you to confront it head on and come up with a creative solution. For example, you could schedule regular check-ins with this person once in the morning and again in the afternoon—or maybe even just once per day. When you walk into a meeting that you know could potentially go on for hours on end, make it a point to tell the person how long you have. You could say, "Oh I'm so excited to meet with you. I have another meeting in thirty minutes so I think we'll have plenty of time to discuss!"

• **GET OVER LUNCHES.** When I worked at the talent agency, my boss was SO cool. She had lunches, drinks, and dinners planned almost every night. I wanted to be just like her. When I started my business I set a lunch every single day with all kinds of people: business contacts, friends, and people I'd met at networking events! And you know what? It was awful. After three weeks of having a lunch every day (following the never eat alone philosophy) I was fat, broke, and ready to yank out my hair from all of the boring conversations I was having over daily lunches. I was wasting hours of my day commuting to and from these lunches and having these awful *nothing* conversations. Sometimes I'd feel like I was going to fall asleep on my pasta because they were just so boring.

If your whole team is getting lunch or breakfast, join them, chat with them, nurture your important relationships, but be judicious and smart about which lunches you take. If my best friend calls me and says she wants to have lunch, I'm most likely going to say yes and be excited to see her. However, if my best friend starts asking to have lunch together every day, I'd suggest something else—on the weekends—something that doesn't have to be smack in the middle of my workday. I can see my personal friends on the weekends and at night. I don't really need to see them during lunchtime. If a professional contact reaches out to have lunch and I think a conversation is needed and that in person would work better than over the phone, I say yes. If I'm unclear what the purpose of the lunch is but feel pressure to say yes, I'll suggest a coffee after work instead. I really hate taking more than an hour to get in the car, drive to a lunch, wait for the person to arrive, eat, wait for the check, and barely make it back to my desk two hours later. Have a lunch plan; your lunch break doesn't need to last that long. Even better, bring your lunch to work. This will save you time and money. Enjoy the quiet time while other people are away from their desks.

SETTING DEADLINES FOR YOURSELF

In chapter three, we talked about organization, prioritization, and maximization. How could you forget, right? Those three lovely words! I want to add on to what we've already discussed about deadlines. If we want to leave the office earlier and feel more in control of our work, deadlines need to be set and assigned, even when they don't *really* exist. Has staying late in the office become routine? Let's try to put a cork in it. Here are a few ideas on how to set deadlines for yourself to slowly start trimming those work hours:

• **IT'S OKAY IF YOU CAN'T FINISH.** In today's fast-paced busy world there is always more work to be done and another to-do list to be made. Get rid of the notion that you have to finish everything that night. Seriously, in my world, that would never happen. As you grow in your business, you'll develop a better understanding of how long certain tasks are going to take you. You want to manage other people's expectations by giving yourself deadlines (provide a few hours' or days' leeway if possible). Be okay with not getting it all done. Some people think that they can't leave the office until they get everything done. You know what happens to those people? They get no sleep, have rings under their eyes, and talk about how they don't sleep. Those are the people who talk about how busy they are. And are they really *that* much further ahead? I have a hard time believing it. You don't need to make yourself miserable and not have a personal life just because you are a hard worker. A hard worker isn't defined by working longer hours, but by what they get done.

• **HAVE A WRAP-UP TIME.** No matter what day it is and how crazy my day gets, 4:30 P.M. is my wrap-up time. That doesn't mean I'm going to leave at 4:30, but it does mean that I'm going to organize my notes from the day, get out any proposals that need to go out by the end of the day, and put all of my pieces of scrap paper into one major to-do list. As I'm putting together the to-do list, I'll just shoot out any urgent or timely e-mails. Getting rid of the mess helps me feel like I'm starting to wind down for the day and putting together all of my notes helps me figure out what I have to do before I leave the office.

• **MAKE A TO-DO LIST AND HAVE A PLAN.** For me, part of having a successful workday is coming up with a personal plan of attack for the day. When I look at my schedule in the morning I immediately notice the things I don't have control of (calls, meetings, deadlines, etc.). I know I cannot be productive during those hours, so I usually try to cross off three things on my to-do list from the previous day before checking my e-mails. I do this in priority order; for me, priority has dollar signs attached to it. If my proposals are out, I go back to my to-do list and if there are any items that need to be done that day, I circle them. I focus on completing those items. If anything random pops up during the day, I make sure to add it to my list. We all wish we could remember everything, but with the amount of information being shared across all of the different channels these days, it's impossible. Write things down all day to make sure you don't forget.

HANG YOUR HAT AND GO HOME!

Staying at work until all hours of the night isn't going to help you, it's not going to help your team, and it's not going to help your work. You have to be ready to walk away from a to-do list. You don't have to work large quantities to churn out high quality. Go to bed. Go home. Do nothing. Do anything but work. This is your life. On a recent episode of *Mad Men*, they said that one guy was such a work-aholic that *when the lights finally go out* he'll probably be in the office. What a sad thought . . .

MAINTAINING WORK-LIFE BALANCE

No matter how hard you try to fight me on this, you need a personal life. You have to know when to hang your hat at the end of the night. You must incorporate work-life balance into your days or else you will be unhappy and go insane. Fair enough?

• **WORKING FROM HOME.** Find a way to be able to log in to your work e-mail from home. Can you forward things to your phone? Even better, is there a laptop that you can bring home that has your work saved on it? Can you access your work e-mails through your personal computer? Being able to work from home will increase your ability to be flexible and flexibility is key. Anything that enables you to leave the office a bit earlier helps your balance.

• **WORKING OUT THREE TIMES PER WEEK.** This isn't something that just magically happens, but a solid workout plan is important. You don't have to join a gym if you don't want to. Experiment with different workouts, try fun classes off Groupon or LivingSocial, go on a walk or run with friends, join a running club. Anything to get active and spend some time taking care of yourself and your body.

• **NO LAPTOP DURING THE WEEKEND.** Try your best to zone out on the weekends. There is no harm in spending a little bit of time on Sunday to check your e-mails and get organized for the next day but make sure you don't go too far into the work zone on the weekends. Saving up your work energy on the weekends will help prevent work burnout during the week. I dare you to remove your e-mail from your phone so you don't have to deal on the weekends. I know, it's tough. But I dare you!

• **HAVE SHUT-OFF NIGHTS AT HOME.** Ivanka Trump (one of my entrepreneurial heroes) and her husband have at least one or two nights per week where they don't allow any work. They also don't allow any television. This forces them to spend time together and actually have conversations. I realize many of you might not be married, but the idea of having a night or two a week when everything just gets turned off is really important. We all know how addicting shows like *Breaking Bad* or *Mad Men* can be when you go home every night and just turn them on. Make yourself spend time with a friend or family member, go for a walk, anything that's not work or television related. Enjoy your time—this is your life!

I want you to start asking yourself, "What are my personal goals? What would make life feel sustainable?" Then, start looking at your calendar and start trying to make those things happen. Maybe I can't control the time I leave work, but I could call my parents on the way to work each day. I can get up thirty minutes earlier and do a twenty-five-minute run two mornings a week. There are ways you can plan these small things to make life sustainable during the time that you do have.

LEARN TO SAY NO

While putting together my research for this book, I had all of my friends over one night. I called it taco and book night. I gave them tacos and they gave me great interviews and information for my book. It was important that I got their insight and learning from their workplace experiences, as we all came up together as young professionals in Hollywood. We were all hanging out, drinking wine, laughing, and telling stories when my friend Shannon looked at me and said, "I have to leave in like fifteen minutes so let's wrap this up soon." Now, Shannon didn't have a mom at home yelling at her to come home, but Shannon takes herself seriously. She knows when to say no and she looks out for herself. When everyone asked, "Why do you need to leave? We are having so much fun!" she looked at them and said, "I need my sleep if I'm going to get up tomorrow, work out, and have a good day at work." It's so important to know when enough is enough, to know when to assert yourself and say no or it's time for me to go home. No one else is looking out for you except you. Take yourself seriously. When you have a deadline, you have to meet it. You must learn to say no and take yourself and what you commit to seriously. You will be done soon enough.

I want us to take back our generation, take back our lives, and take back the notion that we can't be good workers, we can't be hard workers unless we're working sixty-hour weeks way into the night.

I specifically turned these tips into checklists, because I want you to track your progress and flip back to this section. While I don't expect you to follow all of my tips overnight, I do expect you to start following them one at a time. A person who is in control of their work, meets their deadlines, organizes themselves and their workspace, manages expectations, and manages their time is a person who is in control of their job. Remember, you need to be in full control of your job; your job cannot be in control of you.

Before we move on to the personal finance chapter, let's do a recap. I want to make sure you are constantly reminded of the information I shared in this chapter. We talked about time management, the power of the early bird! We talked about ways to productively use your time in the workplace. Some of the key topics and concepts were:

- How to allocate your time between e-mails and outgoing projects
- How to manage people's expectations (your boss's and your clients')
- How saying no is powerful
- How to limit office distractions (I hope you read that section!)
- How to know when it's time to say goodnight and leave the office

I know I'm not the only person who has noticed this busy phenomenon, and I hope as a generation we can acknowledge that it's happening and maybe think to ourselves, "Would it be okay to not be so busy? Could we still feel validated? Could we find other ways to spend our time? Would it be okay to have some downtime?" I'll leave you with that food for thought.

CHAPTER 9

Your Money, Your Finances, Your Life

When I moved out to Los Angeles and got my first job I was barely making any money. I lived paycheck to paycheck. The word *savings* wasn't really part of my vocabulary. I logged online to my bank account numerous times every day, just waiting for some magical increase in funds. I saw negative balances and annoying overdraft fees. I went out to dinner with only $30 in my bank account. I prayed that my bill wouldn't be more than $30. I prayed that my credit card wouldn't get declined. I crossed my fingers that I'd have enough to get me through the entire weekend. We've all been there. You feel like your money—or your lack of money—has control of your life. You try to live like it doesn't matter but it always creeps up on you. Then you are stuck waiting and waiting until that miniscule paycheck comes. I felt like I had no control over my finances, so I spent money when I spent it—and I pretty much ignored my bank accounts. I was knocked out so hard by the real world and my job situation that anything not related to work really got the shaft.

In this chapter, I'll talk about all of the personal things that I neglected. I made the big mistake of pretty much ignoring my finances for the first year or two of my post-college life, so I can relate to exactly what you're going through.

I thought back about my six biggest expenses when I was twenty-two years old and had just moved out to Los Angeles. I was spending my money on:

- **RENT.** One of the biggest expenses you will encounter after graduation, if you aren't living at home, is rent. If you are in a big city, rent can seem like an impossible amount of money to come up with on a monthly basis. In Orlando, Florida, where I went to school, I paid approximately $400 per month for my two bedroom, two bathroom apartment that I shared with a close friend. When I moved to Los Angeles, a one bedroom, one bathroom apartment cost $1350 per month—more than triple what I paid in college. The beginning of the month was always stressful because I knew I had to come up with the money. I typically got paid twice per month and more than one of my checks would go solely to rent. It was also difficult to remember to pay rent at the beginning of every month. It was just one more thing to remember and I often had yellow notices taped to my door, reminding me that it was time to pay up or move out.

- **FOOD.** I rarely went grocery shopping and I never brought a lunch to work. I always spent money on food. Typically, I'd eat no breakfast (or have chicken noodle soup from across the street for breakfast—weird, I know); get food from somewhere close to the office for lunch; and go out for dinner (either by myself or with friends). For some reason, I had a thing for Wendy's chili. I never even liked Wendy's growing up! But on my way home from work there was a Wendy's across the street and I'd sit in the drive-thru line just craving that hot chili . . .

- **DRINKS.** We had lots of drinks. Happy-hour drinks; post-happy hour drinks; weekend brunch all-you-can-drink Mimosas at the Saddle Ranch; and Friday and Saturday night drinks, which were a bit more excessive than the rest of the week. And remember, I was in LA, so each drink (my drink of choice is the dirty martini) would run me about $13—and they added up!

• **NORDSTROM AND FOREVER 21.** I know, I'm a sucker for Nordstrom— not the super expensive stuff, but their juniors section. Since I didn't take very good care of myself and neglected important things like laundry, I would run out of clothes and then just go buy new ones. At the time, it made sense. I'd buy piles of new dresses, tops, and pants. Not to mention, I was constantly gaining weight from all the eating out, so I kept buying looser clothing.

• **COFFEE.** To get through my intense workdays, I spent way too much money on coffee. I bought a Starbucks on the way to work, a Coffee Bean coffee at lunch, and sometimes another Starbucks on the way home if I had a whole night ahead of me. Even if you are like me and just ordering iced coffees, $2 each, that's more than $6 a day in coffee. Over the span of a week that's $42 just in coffee expenses! Looking back, we had coffee in the office, why didn't I just drink that for free? Again, something I would tell my twenty-two-year-old self.

• **WEDDINGS.** I moved to Los Angeles at twenty-two from Florida and, instantly, three of my closest friends from home got engaged. Do you know how much it costs to be in a wedding? In order to be in the wedding, you have to purchase several plane tickets home for the bridal shower, bachelorette party, and wedding, and spend tons of money on the dresses (these cost about $250 each, on average).

Earlier in the book we talked about how fast things move after graduation. Your finances are no different. You leave college six pence none the richer. If you are lucky, some aunts and uncles send you checks in the mail for graduation. But other than that, you are on your own. Your parents are trying to hide their excitement. They are finally able to cut you off! They aren't paying your car insurance, your cell phone bill—nothing! While they celebrate, you start to feel sorry for yourself. It just doesn't add up. You make nothing and you are supposed to be doing everything. How is that supposed to work? I can feel your frustration through the pages. The biggest change you have to understand after college graduation is that no one is babysitting you anymore. You are responsible for setting your own boundaries, and that's not easy in any sense of the word. Even if you went out of state for college, you still had professors, counselors, coaches, sorority presidents, and school administrators tracking your every move. Now, you are completely on your own—and it's scary. When it comes to managing your finances and being fiscally responsible, you are going to have to become a very cautious decider of what you do with your money, aware of what you're spending, and savvy—as you likely won't be bringing home a huge paycheck right after college. Luckily for you, I was once financially reckless and made the bad decisions that you don't have to make. I'm going to provide you with some rules to follow for financial sanity in your personal life. I'm also going to provide some great information from financial experts on savings strategies, 401(k) retirement plans, and how to gear up for your first round of big-kid taxes. Like everything else in this book, I learned how to organize my finances, track my spending, and take care of myself financially through trial and error. Here are some lessons I learned the hard way that I'd love to pass on:

RENT RULES

First of all, you have to live somewhere you can afford. I spoke with Alexa von Tobel, founder and CEO of LearnVest.com and author of *Financially Fearless*, and she reiterated that your rent should only cost 30 to 35 percent of your total income each month. "For example, if you make $1000 each month after taxes, your rent should be $300 or less each month," Alexa explains. She also warns that it's critical to get this right or you're going to automatically be in financial trouble. Make sure you do the math before signing a lease. The last thing you want to do is live somewhere you can't afford and be stressed out about it.

Great options to consider are finding a roommate, either online or through a friend, or living at home, if that's a possibility, and trying to save some money. I know a ton of my former Intern Queen ambassadors are from the New Jersey area and are living at home while working their first, second, or third jobs in New York City to save money so they can eventually make that move into the city. They commute in every day and save money by living at home. If you are going to live at home, that's a great idea—for now. Make sure you don't get stuck there. Have a plan and timeline in your mind. Perhaps you save money for one year and then find your own place. You don't want to live with Mom and Dad forever.

When you go to furnish your place look for used furniture so you don't spend a ton of money furnishing an already expensive place. Also look for places that are close to public transportation, in safe neighborhoods, and are rent controlled, meaning they aren't going to push the rent up every year.

FOOD AND DRINK RULES

When you get that first job, it's natural to want to be social—and by all means, you SHOULD be social. This is the time when you are going to meet that next set of friends, the after-college friends. You are going to want to do everything, go everywhere, and meet everyone—and I want you to do that. BUT there is a financially responsible way to do it. When it comes to food and drinks, I suggest holding yourself responsible for the following:

• **LET YOURSELF EAT OUT TWICE A WEEK FOR DINNER.** Once during the week, and once on the weekends. You can still go to meals with people, but just order something small or get a drink. Look at the menu before you go so that you know what you're getting yourself into. I can't tell you how many times I've agreed to group dinners with friends, show up starving, and then realize nothing on the menu is under $40. If you need to cut back on spending eat beforehand so that you can just order a small side salad or a cocktail. When you eat out typically the portions are pretty large, so getting in the habit of sharing entrees with friends is always a good idea. Also, try to stick to one drink at dinners, as the check can really start to pile up and you don't want to get yourself into a "splitting the bill" situation with people who've had a ton of drinks. You can still be social, go out with your friends, and order a side salad if you want, you just don't need to spend the money on another meal out.

• **LEARN HOW TO COOK YOUR OWN FOOD.** Ask your mom. Buy a cookbook. Whatever you need to do to start making meals for yourself. You will save boatloads of money this way. When I graduated, someone got me a subscription to the *Every Day with Rachael Ray* magazine and I followed her thirty-minute meals to the T. It was a random gift but it really paid off and helped me to save money.

• **BRING YOUR LUNCH.** During your first job, you probably won't have much time to escape during the lunch hour. Every once in a while it's fine to go out for lunch but try to bring in food as much as possible. This will save your wallet and your waistline.

• **DON'T SPLIT THE BILL IF YOU DIDN'T EAT.** Many young people at those dreaded group dinners end up splitting the bill when they hardly ordered anything. It's a quick way for an $8 dinner to turn into a $30 dinner. Splitting the bill is great when everyone orders similar amounts of food or drinks. But if you aren't drinking and everyone else is, don't split the bill.

- **THE DRINKS GET PRICEY—BE AWARE.** You will probably be doing a fair amount of drinking with your coworkers, which can lead to inappropriate comments, hookups, and sharing confidential information. The drinks will create a hole in your wallet and they aren't great for your liver or your weight. My best advice to avoid this getting out of hand is to build yourself some sort of budget. How much are you allowing yourself to spend on food and drinks each week? Doing this will cause you to really look at the places you are going and the prices they charge before you commit.

- **FIND THE FREEBIES!** Kellie from Ogilvy & Mather in Chicago says, "Most cities have free events—festivals, concerts, food tastings, and more great events—to take advantage of." She also encourages her peers to share cabs with friends when possible and keep close track of personal spending habits.

CREDIT CARDS

When I graduated college, I had a debit card but no credit card. My parents got me one of those prepaid Visa Buxx cards where they added money to it. Allowance if you will, but it was more like a gift card. I really had no credit, so in order to get a credit card, I walked into my Wells Fargo bank and gave them a check for $1,000. I basically created my own credit line. They held onto my $1,000 for about a year and a half and then eventually gave it back and increased my credit limit. If you can't get a credit card, this is a great way to establish your own line of credit and prove to the bank that you can be responsible.

I asked Alexa von Tobel what she thought about young people having credit cards. She said, "A credit card is a wonderful tool if you use it properly." Here are some tips on how to use that credit card properly:

• **USE IT TO BUILD CREDIT.**
Alexa says that you only need to spend $5 to $10 per month to start building credit. She says you must pay off the entire balance all of the time. She says to pay twice a month.

• **PROMPT PAYMENTS.** Make payments on your bills on time. No matter what.

• **CHECK YOUR CREDIT SCORE.** Use sites like FreeCreditReport.com and AnnualCreditReport.com to do this. You're allowed to get one free report every year. Be aware of what your credit score looks like.

• **THROW OUT MAIL ADVERTISEMENTS.** Ignore most of the stuff that comes in the mail. You aren't going to want most of those cards. At this point in your life, focus on building credit on one credit card.

• **AVOID CREDIT CARDS FOR EVERY STORE.** You don't need a different credit card for each of your favorite stores in the mall. In fact, I'd advise against those cards. Avoid department store credit cards as those just promote more shopping and debt!

• **KEEP A LOW LIMIT FOR YOURSELF.** Why put yourself in potential credit card debt danger? I suggest creating a limit of no more than $1,500. Why would you need any more than that? You can always go back and raise the limit in the future. I have friends in thousands of dollars' worth of credit card debt because they got excited when they were in their early twenties and never paid off the cards they kept getting and using.

• **LEARN TO SAY NO.** We talked about this concept earlier in the book. I want to reiterate it: Everyone is going to ask you to do everything all of the time. If you say yes to everything you'll go broke. They will invite you to take a limo or party bus out for someone's birthday, go to a club, go to a bar, go to a concert—you have to learn to say no. If you need to tell people that you'll meet them after dinner and just have drinks—that's fine!

• **CREATE A BUDGET.** Creating a budget for yourself is key to living a financially sound life in your early twenties. Treat yourself like a business. Take your finances seriously and it will create a stress-free environment. The closer you stick to the budget the better off you will be.

HOW TO CREATE A BUDGET

....

- Start a new Excel or Google Doc sheet, and name it My Personal Budget.
- Determine how much you make, how much you want to spend, and how much you want to save.
- Make a list of rows going down. What do you spend money on? You already know what my budget looked like. Now, look at yours. You want to create categories, such as Rent, Utilities, Cell Phone, Insurance, Food, Shopping, Drinks, Entertainment, Parking, et cetera.
- Make different columns for each month, and give yourself a budgeted amount for each of the categories above. Make sure the budgeted amount is less than what you actually make!
- At the end of every month, go into your online bank statement and write down what you actually spent, and then compare it to your budgeted amount. Just being aware of what you are spending is going to help you control your budget. It's important to put a date in your calendar (I prefer Sundays) to go over the numbers.

GIFT CARDS

Gift cards are great, just remember to actually use them. Some people (like myself) keep them piled up and have the "once I use them they are gone" fear. Get over it and use them wisely. If you have a stack of gift cards lying around the house, put them in one spot. Make a list of things you need. Can you get any of them at those stores? Give yourself a gift card day and happy spending!

GROUPONS

It's crazy that I can call a section *Groupons* and everyone will know what I mean. Groupon didn't even exist a few years back. Sites like LivingSocial, Thrillist, Groupon, and Jetsetter put an interesting value add on the table. On one hand, they inform you about new cool places to try and fun activities to do with groups of friends, and of course, I love that it's discounted. However, it's kind of like shopping the sales rack. Do you really need that stuff? Some stuff makes sense. For example, getting a Groupon to your favorite restaurant to cut down your tab might make sense. Getting a Groupon for an expensive workout class, just because it's on sale, seems to make less sense.

Websites like Yelp often have specials when you check in. I went to dinner the other night and we got two free flatbreads because two of us checked in at the restaurant on Yelp. Again, look up where you are going beforehand so that you can check for any special deals. There's plenty to be found for the savvy consumer.

CASH

If you live in a city where you need a car, the one thing you are always going to need cash for is valet parking. And the only time you need to valet is when street parking or large parking lots are unavailable. Otherwise, I rarely need cash and try not to have it on me. I'm the person who always spends cash when I have it. I suggest always carrying $10 in your wallet, but other than that, put it where you can't touch it (directly)—in the bank! If you are at a dinner and you put everything on your credit card and your friends give you cash, go to the bank immediately. Just because you have it doesn't mean you should spend it.

BILLS

Earlier in the book, I spoke about having a system and mapping things out. You also need to develop manageable systems for handling bills. Get in the habit of paying all of your bills online. You want your bills to be organized and uniform. You don't want to ever miss bills. I suggest having a file in your e-mail labeled Personal where you can store any of your passwords or log-ins for your bills. Try to keep them as uniform as possible by using the same username and passwords for each one. Sign up for automatic withdrawals for as many bills as you can so that you don't risk missing a bill. Make sure you are aware of which day of the month that company will be taking money out of your account and mark it on your calendar. You want to give yourself a day or so to make sure you have the available funds. I also suggest setting up a back-up account with your bank, so should there be insufficient funds in your primary account the bank can automatically pull from a savings account to cover the charges. This way you don't get charged for any mishaps.

The quickest way to go into debt is from late fees and shut-off fees. Make sure you track all of the due dates for your bills. Pay them a week ahead of time if possible.

If there are any paper bills make sure you have a system at home. Once bills come in that need to be paid via phone call or check, have a place where you leave them until they are paid. Don't hide them—you need to remind yourself daily that the bill is due. Common bills that you should be prepared to pay once you graduate are

• **ELECTRICITY AND GAS.** Try to conserve energy as much as possible. Only use the air conditioning and heat when you need it. Shut the lights off before you leave the house. And make sure you don't leave for vacation without turning off your lights and air conditioning. Being aware of your electric and gas bills will help to keep them low.

• **CABLE, INTERNET, AND PHONE.** (If you pay for a home phone—most grads just use their cell phones.) Sometimes it makes your cable bill cheaper when you add a phone; this makes no sense, but look into it. If you have crazy cable packages (like I do) so that you can watch shows like *Game of Thrones* and *Shameless* (like I do), only keep those channels when you need them. When those shows aren't on the air, you can call the cable company and have the channels removed. This will save you some money on your bill. You might also avoid cable entirely and just get a Netflix or Hulu Plus subscription.

• **INSURANCE.** Most of you will get covered. If you are a 1099 worker (contractor) you'll likely have to cover your own health insurance. Make sure you look into this and make it a priority. Do some comparison shopping. What is the best plan for you? Remember, everyone needs health insurance. You want to make sure you are covered for a rainy day.

• **CELL PHONE.** It seems old school but pay attention to your plan. Since you are going to be in the office all day, you might not need your cell phone minutes all day. Also, if you are at a job where you must use your own phone, you might want to ask your employer if they would be able to compensate you for any of your minutes or another part of your bill.

You want to keep records of all of your bills. Most of you won't have big filing cabinets, so just grabbing a large decorative box from IKEA or something works just fine. Buy some file folders and make a folder for all of your bills. If you are paying with your credit card for most things you won't have to keep your receipts. I suggest keeping receipts when you pay in cash, as you'll have no way to track that with your online banking. Create a file folder for yourself for bills that have already been paid. As soon as I pay a bill, I write the date on it, and add it to a folder that I have labeled To be Filed. The other labeled folders I have is my To Handle folder with all of the bills that need to be paid for the month.

Experts say that you should keep copies of your bills on hand for three years. Nowadays, everything is online so you should be able to keep organized copies in computer files.

ONLINE SOLUTIONS

• **VENMO.** I recently started using the app Venmo, which allows me to pay my friends and family for anything at anytime. It hooks up easily with a credit card or bank account and there are no extra charges to use it.

• **BANK TRANSFERS.** Several of my friends bank with Bank of America so they can easily reimburse one another through their online banking system. Since I don't have the same bank as they do, I use Venmo to transfer money.

• **LEARNVEST.COM.** The brainchild of Alexa von Tobel, several young people use this tool to manage their money and their savings. One of our former ambassadors, Danielle, says, "I use Learnvest.com because it breaks down everything really well and is visually appealing. It links straight to my bank account and credit cards so I can see exactly where my money is going. It helps me budget and know when I can and cannot splurge."

• **QUICKBOOKS ONLINE.** This famous financial software recently became available online. I use this to manage my personal monthly expenses and my business expenses. Managing my money every month makes it very easy to organize my taxes at the end of the year and to track my spending.

• **MINT**.com. Another former ambassador, Jackie, says, "Mint.com makes it really easy to keep track of your finances. The bottom line is don't spend it if you don't have it!"

401(K) AT WORK

Retirement saving is very important for young professionals to be knowledgeable about and aware of. I called my CPA, Steve Rousso, CEO of Stephen M. Rousso and Associates in Sherman Oaks, California, to pick his brain about what young people need to know about retirement. He provided me with these four helpful tips:

• Find out if your company offers any options for retirement accounts. Some companies have plans where the employer is the only one who contributes to the plan. Steve says that with most company 401(k) plans, the more employees that participate in the 401(k), the more the employer is able to put in the plan. "Employers typically encourage their employees to put money into a 401(k) by offering a match of some kind. You should almost *always* take advantage of employer match. If you don't you are leaving money on the table." Steve says even if the match is only 1 to 3 percent, take it, it's worth it.

• If your company doesn't have a 401(k), you have two choices: You can go to the bank and ask for an IRA, or you can invest in the stock market.

Steve says, "I would discourage young people from going to a bank, but each person has to be comfortable about how they invest their money. My advice to young people is to stretch your comfort zone when it comes to investing your money in the stock market. That money is going to go in now and be invested over many years to come. Therefore, it can recover from the inevitable changes in the stock market. I really encourage my clients to put their money in the stock market—even though it might not be the most comfortable place. There has never been a twenty-year period where someone lost their principal by investing in the stock market. They will get killed with inflation if you go only to the bank for investment." Steve says that getting comfortable with investing means acknowledging that money can go up and money can go down. "When the market goes down, it's a buying opportunity."

The final thought Steve left me with was that he thinks the number one mistake young people make is that they don't think about retirement early enough. Use the information above to start thinking about your retirement plan and have a conversation with your employer or bank.

YOUR SAVINGS ACCOUNT PLAN AND STRATEGY

When you get that first job, you'll probably have two main bank accounts that you are focused on—your personal savings account and your personal checking account. You might have a little bit in your personal savings already. And you probably put your biweekly paychecks into and do most of your transaction and purchases from your checking account. This works and makes sense. I want you to take it one step further by creating a system for yourself. How frequently will you put money into savings? How much money do you want in your checking account before it's time to transfer some to savings? You should always put at least 10 percent of your check into your savings account right away, and pretend you never had it. This is the only way that a savings account will ever grow.

PREPARE FOR YOUR FIRST ROUND OF BIG-KID TAXES

For this brief tax discussion, I turned again to Steve Rousso, my CPA, to help us develop a better understanding for how we organize our taxes. Steve encourages young people to get knowledgeable about these things. The IRS offers free tax preparation courses if you are interested. You can also visit IRS.gov to get more information on how much you owe. Some websites with great information on taxes also include TurboTax.com, HRBlock.com, or TaxACT.com. If your family uses a CPA it might be a good idea to have a conversation with him. Steve says, "Recent grads don't necessary have to rely on someone to file their first tax return. It might be so simple that they don't need any professional help. That being said, don't do your taxes on your own unless you are comfortable with it."

He goes on. "If you only have a W2, you should be able to do your own tax return. You probably aren't going to get above the standard deduction. You can't itemize your possessions because you don't own the real estate. Life gets more complicated when you acquire real estate. You should think about help down the line with tax preparations and the deductions that come from mortgage interest and charitable contributions."

This book is all about taking control of the chaos that becomes your life after college when you dive head first into that first, second, or third job. Being financially responsible, tracking your expenses, being aware of what you are spending, understanding how to save money, and learning about 401(k) plans and taxes isn't something covered in most college courses. This information definitely wasn't covered my senior year of college.

I remember being frazzled by my finances and feeling so overwhelmed. Hopefully, this section really broke each expense down for you and provided some helpful tips on how to save money and be more aware of where your money goes. We are all going to get the big paychecks that we deserve someday. I have no doubt that if you're reading this book, you are on a path to success. But until that day comes, we must be mindful about our money, manage it properly, and spend conservatively—as we never know what tomorrow will bring.

CHAPTER **10**

Time to Get Personal

When I moved across the country to Los Angeles after graduation I used Craigslist (everyone's favorite) to find an apartment and a roommate. I moved in with a girl named Ainsley. She lived in a two bedroom, two bathroom apartment in West Hollywood, a popular place for young twentysomethings to move after college. Ainsley was gorgeous—supermodel gorgeous. She was tall with huge fake boobs and skinny as could be. Ainsley had a closet full of party dresses in every color—I'd never seen anything like it. In Orlando, where I finished college, we wore jeans and tank tops out at night. Ainsley would never be caught dead in jeans and a tank top on a Saturday night.

My first night out in Los Angeles, my friend Shannon (from a past internship) and I had no idea where to go or what was "cool." We went to a club that had a short line called Basque. After seeing Ainsley's closet, I knew we needed dresses. The two of us sported nearly identical Forever 21 short, cotton dresses and gold jeweled necklaces. We attempted Jessica Simpson curls; it sort of worked. We went out, took Patron shots, got drunk, and came back to my place. Ainsley was just getting ready to go out as we were coming home. She always went to the coolest after-parties. But we were tired! It was 2 A.M. We didn't want to go to an after-party. Ainsley asked us what club we went to. She gasped. "Don't *ever* tell *anyone* you went there. OMG. That's *so* embarrassing!" And then she left the apartment. Shannon and I sat there dumbfounded.

Over the course of our stay together, Ainsley taught me to shop at Image for party dresses, to always carry a clutch bag, to never pay for a drink, and how to meet boys in line for clubs and sit with them at their tables. Although we never made it to any of her after-parties, because we were too tired. A few months into our stay together, Ainsley told me she was moving in with her boyfriend and that the property managers were turning our building into condos. I had to move out. Ugh. My dad had flown out to LA to move me in (in June) and now I'd have to move out by myself and find a place to live (in October). So I'd only been in my place for four months! I was annoyed and I wanted my own place. With my hectic job and crazy current roommate, I couldn't deal with another.

I found another place in West Hollywood and moved in right away. One Saturday night, my friends and I went out to an assistant's birthday party. I'm telling you, it was *always* someone's birthday. We went to a dive bar in Hollywood (I think it still exists) called The 3 Clubs. We immediately went to the bar and did our usual—Patron shots. We danced our behinds off, took more shots, and then went back to my place. I had just moved in and apparently wasn't sober enough to remember which apartment was mine. My friends *love* telling this story.

Apparently, we just started knocking on strangers' doors until we found a door where my key worked. All I remember is the next morning waking up to the doorbell ringing loudly on repeat. Who could that be? I rolled over. Gross! My fingers touched something gooey! My eyes finally opened. I fell asleep next to my Swedish meatball Lean Cuisine—yuck! I stumbled out of bed, tripped over my platform stilettos from the night before, and just looked at the chaos that was my room. How did my Lean Cuisine get all over the room? I rummaged through my junk to find some sweats to throw on so that I could see who was at the door. Uh oh. I felt like I was going to throw up. I poked my head out of the door. Two irritated-looking men stood with a ton of wrapped furniture behind them. "Ma'am, we've been ringing the doorbell for twenty minutes. We have your furniture here. Do you want us to set it up?" I didn't know what was going to come out of my mouth. "Umm . . . no," I said quickly. "Just leave it inside." (I pointed to the main room.) "I'll be in the other room." I propped the door open for them and ran back into my room to pass out again. I needed to sleep this off.

I woke up hours later to find my new couches standing on their sides and still fully wrapped in plastic. I felt like such an asshole. What was I doing? I had a lot of work to do.

During my first few years on the job, that was the disaster that was my personal life. I was my own last priority. I was a mess. My hair was always half-done, I never worked out, I was too big for most of my fitted clothes, my bills went unpaid, my laundry piled up, my room wasn't clean, and I ate out every night. Gross, right? I didn't even pay attention to my credit card or my cash flow or what I was spending money on. Personal errands never happened, and I would just go buy new clothes when I ran out. I was trying so hard to keep up with the social aspect of my newfound job and the actual work I had to do that I forgot about myself. I let myself go—in every sense of the phrase. I didn't understand that if I didn't make myself a priority, no one else would.

Here's how to manage yourself, how to make yourself a priority, and how to do the things that enable you to do you.

ERRANDS

You might be asking yourself why I would include a section on errands in this book. Well, when I started my first job one of the biggest problems I had was that I had no time to get anything done. I went from having all of the time in the world while I was at school to rushing around and having time for nothing at my first job. I especially didn't know how to make time for myself and the errands I needed to get done. Even though I had a big new job, I still needed to be a normal person and go to the bank, the gym, the post office, and keep my personal life together. But no one told me how to do this. If you ever want to feel like you truly have it all together, you need to learn to make time for yourself. You have to block out time to get errands done. Here are some tips on how to manage all of the errands that you might need to run:

• **THE BANK.** Obviously, if you don't have direct deposit, you'll need to head to the bank frequently. Also, if you need to get money out of an ATM, save a little and go to your bank ATM.

• **THE DRY CLEANERS.** Certain items in your wardrobe will need to be dry cleaned. You'll also need to determine if you are going to do your own laundry or take advantage of the fluff-n-fold services. If you live in a big city and you don't have a washing machine that's convenient to get to, fluff-n-fold might make more sense. For example, my younger brother lives in New York City. His washer/dryer situation is nonexistent. Once a week, on his way to work, he drops his clothes off at a dry cleaner and picks up his stuff on the way home. Another friend, Shannon, doesn't have a convenient situation but prefers to save money and do her own wash. She picks one day a week, typically a weeknight or the weekend, and brings a stack of work or a book and plans to sit at the Laundromat and do her work. She plans her time and makes the most of it.

• **THE POST OFFICE.** Obviously, you won't have to go to the post office that often. But there will be times where you need to mail gifts, letters, et cetera. I suggest buying a sheet of stamps to keep at your desk at work.

• **THE DMV.** At some point, you will need to get a new license at the DMV for the city you've moved to. I like to drive a little farther to go to the DMV so that I don't have to wait in the long Hollywood lines.

• **DOCTOR'S APPOINTMENTS.** Doctor's appointments are really important. You need to see your doctor once a year. If you are female you need your annual exams. And you need to go to the dentist. I would go to the doctor before the workday starts. So get ready for those 7 A.M. appointments or look for half days at the office, because you usually can't go during the regular workweek.

• **THE GYM.** When I moved to Los Angeles, a friend recommended a local trainer known as Trainer Nicki. She was known for great, tough, Jillian Michaels–style workouts while being extremely cost effective. She also had her own equipment so you didn't have to pay for a gym membership. I started working out with Nicki and it did wonders for my body, my attitude, and my self-esteem. She charged me under $40 per hour and we would meet up at local parks to work out. I found this to be a great release at the end of a long workday.

I can't stress how important some kind of workout is to your first, second, or third job lifestyle. Not only is it the obvious healthy choice, but it also helps with stress, balance, anger, confusion, depression, and focus. A first real job is a challenge and a change. You are going to deal with an entirely new set of emotions. You are also going to deal with a new set of people. Some of them are going to seem psychotic and you are going to have to deal with them. And guess what one of your best secret weapons is? Your workout. Find a cheap gym near you and find a time that makes sense to go. It could be in the morning or in the evenings but going only on the weekends isn't enough. Some people even go to the gym during their lunch break if it's close enough. If you aren't a gym person, decide what your workout plan is going to be. Will you take hip-hop dance classes at a local studio? Will you hike a few times per week? Join a community sports team? The goal I'm giving you is to work out at least three times during the week and once on the weekends. When I started my first job, I didn't work out and I had no place to release the stress and negative energy. When I started to work out I would literally punch through my problems in kickboxing classes or spin through them in the mornings. It was such a healthy release. Studies show that the biggest personal factor in determining happiness is your health and working out keeps your health on track. Healthy people are about 20 percent happier on average than people who live unhealthy lifestyles.

YOUR SOCIAL LIFE

After talking with several of my alumni ambassadors who are now in their first, second, and third years of their jobs, I realized I had to include a section on FOMO. I thought FOMO was just something my friends and I suffered from but I heard about this issue from at least seven of the girls I interviewed. What is FOMO? FOMO stands for the fear of missing out and apparently it affects more people than I thought. Here are some pointers on how to deal:

• **GET OVER IT.** I know that's blunt but you can't be everywhere and do everything. Trust me, if there were a way, I would do it! You can't live your life scared you will miss out on things. If you do, you won't ever have time to relax and rejuvenate.

• **SAYING NO IS OKAY.** You can't say yes to everything. In fact, challenge yourself, make yourself say no to one invitation every week. Tell your friend you'll make it up to her; you just have to have some *you* time.

• **YOU MUST SLEEP.** Eight hours of sleep every night is a great goal. With your new job, I'm not sure you can swing that, but again, it's a great goal to have. You need your sleep if you are going to be running a mile a minute at work.

FRIENDS

Friends are important. I think when you graduate and move away from home friends become even more important. You no longer have the safety net of your family nearby and so now you rely on your friends to be that safety net for you, that comfort zone. I think friendships in your twenties are confusing, chaotic, and special. Someone once told me that you want to make the kinds of friends who will help you move or drive you to the airport. They meant that you want to make friends who will hang out with you in the most unglamorous of situations. I've had the same group of five close friends since I moved to Los Angeles. These are friends from my internships (of course). And yes, we would do anything for each other and we have. We've been through a lot together. Sad times: scary hospital visits, family members passing away, parents getting sick; and happy times: getting promoted at work, birthdays, book deals, and other happy celebrations. They are the kinds of friends who won't air my dirty laundry—no matter how dirty it gets. They are the friends who truly support me through all of my endeavors. Together we're there for each other no matter what.

From my experiences and what I've learned over the years, when you make good friends like I've been lucky enough to make, you have to see them and spend time together. You have to make them a priority. These aren't the kind of friends who you put off, flake out on, or disregard. These friends are like family. Here are some pointers on how we all manage to stay in the loop, stay connected, and spend time together even though we're all *so busy* (that busy word again!).

- **E-MAIL CHAINS.** We try to make plans via group e-mail chains and update one another on what's going on. We don't generally see each other during the week (we're out networking, enjoying some quiet time, or getting work done), but we do communicate during the week via group e-mails. And some get pretty fun. Another reason why you should separate your personal e-mails from work e-mails.

- **GROUP TEXTS.** When we need to make last-minute plans or text someone a picture of something funny, we go right to the group text. It's a major time saver!

- **TRYING NEW RESTAURANTS.** We all enjoy trying new things so lately we've made it a goal to try at least one new restaurant together every four weeks. We always take advantage of Restaurant Week in Los Angeles where they have discounts at the places that would normally be too expensive for us to go.

- **BRUNCHES.** If everyone has plans all weekend (Friday and Saturday night) we'll all meet up for a Sunday brunch to have catch-up time.

- **BI-YEARLY TRIPS.** We've made it a goal to go on one big group trip every other year. We'll all save up our money and our vacation time and do an all-inclusive trip. In fact, the day I turn my book in I'm headed to Cabo with my Los Angeles friends. We all try to be financially responsible, so this trip was planned two years ago and was paid for six months ago. We all saved up, coordinated our calendars, and gave our jobs plenty of notice. When you work together to plan, anything can happen.

- **MAKE TIME TOGETHER A PRIORITY.** My schedule isn't easy and I know yours isn't either. In order to make sure that I actually see my friends and spend time with them, we plan ahead. I let them know what weekends I'll be out of town and they let me know when they'll be busy, have family visiting, or just won't be around. Since we're all so busy and wrapped up in our jobs, it's important that we make a group effort to coordinate schedules and actually plan something when everyone is around.

• **CELEBRATE WHENEVER POSSIBLE.** It's important to always celebrate the good times. My friends and I are very good at that. Whenever we have a reason to celebrate, we try to go out or get together and have a good time. If someone is on a money diet that week, we'll go to one of our apartments and order pizza or have a game night. Everyone goes on a money diet at some point!

FAMILY AND FRIENDS FROM HOME

I'm very close with my family (mom, dad, younger brother), but we all live in different parts of the country (different time zones). I'm in Los Angeles, my parents are in Florida, and my brother lives in New York. For a family that is spread across the United States, we actually do a great job of making sure to see each other at least every few months in a different city. For example, my parents came to visit last December. I planned a trip home to Florida with my brother in May so we were all together there. Everyone came to New York in July for the Intern Queen party and my brother came to visit me in October. We seem to get around!

I'm also very close with a handful of friends from Florida, high school friends. We've battled with time zones and work schedules for years. Now that I run my own business, I have more freedom in terms of when I can call my family and friends. And trust me—I call them frequently. But when I had my first job, it was always tricky. Earlier in the book, I explained the time zone conundrum. Here are some tips on how to stay in touch with your family and friends when you aren't living near them:

• **WEEKLY ROUTINES.** My friend Sammy has a system with her dad. For years, they've stuck to speaking once a week on Wednesday evenings. Sammy goes out of her way to make sure she and her father connect every Wednesday. Come up with one day of the week that you will talk to your family. Start there and try to stick to it—no matter what. Routine is important when it comes to staying in touch.

• **CAR TIME = PHONE TIME.** Whenever I'm in the car, I use that time to call my family, my friends from home, and any other personal friend I haven't spoken to in a while. Of course, I do this either on speaker phone or using a hands-free device. This enables me to get back to almost everyone, every week. Even if I'm only leaving them a funny voicemail message, at least they know I'm putting in the effort. Several of my friends also use this method for talking to their families and friends from across the country. They all said they spend lots of time in the car on their Bluetooths speaking to the 'rents.

• **FACEBOOK GROUPS.** Several of my former Intern Queen ambassadors told me that they use Facebook groups to stay in touch with their friends and family from home. They are private groups so they just post status updates all of the time. I thought this was a cute idea!

• **TAKE A LUNCHTIME LOOP.** Need some fresh air during your workday? Take a walk around the block at lunch and phone a family member or a friend.

• **USE WEEKENDS TO GET CAUGHT UP.** If you find yourself having a hard time reaching your family or friends from home during the week, use your weekend time for catch up. Wake up early and sit in bed with your phone. This can be a mix of relax time and catch up time for you. You can also FaceTime with friends or family from home.

• **CHAT WHILE GETTING READY.** If you are a multitasker, this might work for you. My friend Shannon, who works in television, says, "I'll sit on my floor curling my hair in the mornings and FaceTime with my sister or my mom and dad. You do what you can to stay in touch."

RELATIONSHIPS

Most people go through a few different relationships over the course of their first, second, and third jobs. It's a hectic situation—I've been there. On one hand, you want to work your butt off and do everything and anything you can to get ahead. On the other hand, all you want to do is go hang out with this special someone and throw on comfy pants and order Chinese food. I get it! When I think about what I've learned from different relationships over the years (especially those I had during my first year at my job), this is the advice I would give (warning: I am not a relationships expert):

• **IF THEY AREN'T GIVING YOU THE TIME OF DAY, LOSE THEM.** I dated guys who told me they were into me or wanted to take me out and then fell off the face of the earth. I remember trying to text them or track them down. They were clearly uninterested. Guys don't have to physically chase you down but if they want to spend time with you, you will know. If it's a guessing game, it's probably a no.

• **YOU ARE YOURSELF AND ONLY YOURSELF.** When you move to a new city and make new friends and meet new people, it can get confusing. You revisit who you are and learn new things about yourself. Just remember that if someone doesn't like *you* for *you*, they aren't for you.

• **NO GAMES.** If you played games with the opposite sex in high school or college, that's fine. You probably had nothing better to do (been there). But now you are a young professional, you have a job, and you're trying to really take yourself seriously for the first time. You don't have time to play games. You read the busy chapter. No games. Who has time for that? And what's the point?

• **WHEN IT'S RIGHT, MAKE THE TIME.** If you find someone special, don't let them slip away. Don't make them feel bad, don't ditch them at night, don't stay out too late partying with coworkers and make them question your loyalty. When you find the right one, treat them like the right one.

• **BALANCE IS STILL KEY.** When you are in a relationship and also dealing with an intense job, you have to think about balance. Will it be easy? No, but it's definitely possible and, if you found the right person, well worth it. Be aware of how you spend your time and make sure you are still devoting the necessary time to the workplace, networking events, and your personal friends.

• **THE LITTLE THINGS COUNT.** If you know you are going to have a busy week at work and you won't be able to see your significant other—do something nice for him or her. Do something to reassure them. Make plans for the following weekend. Send them a little note. Leave them a small gift. These little things mean more than you know and in a world filled with crazy bosses and long hours, it will go a long way.

TAKE A LITTLE TIME FOR YOURSELF

I've mentioned this several times in this book, but when I graduated I didn't understand the importance of "me" time. It sounds cheesy, but I've come to realize it's one of the most important things I can do for myself. When I graduated, life was about my boss, my social life, and my friends. Everything else slipped through the cracks, including me. I've already explained how this affected my appearance, but it also affected my brain and my mind-set. It took me a few months to figure this out. The things that keep me the most balanced are:

• **GYM ROUTINE.** I've already mentioned this, but a solid workout plan keeps me balanced. For me, it's going to my local Piloxing class, an upbeat mix of Pilates and kickboxing. It's a positive way to release my energy and frustrations (I build up a lot of them).

• **SPA DAYS.** Let's be honest, I can't afford to go to the spa as much as I'd like, so often I'll create my own. I try to do this once every other week. This is a girly thing, I admit, but every other week I'll pull out all of my lotions, potions, cotton swabs, and face and hair masks, and I'll give myself a spa evening. I'll do a deep cleanse, dim the lights in the bathroom, light candles, play meditation music on my phone, and just relax. After the shower, I'll put on a face mask and just make myself lie on the floor surrounded by blankets and comfy pillows. If I fall asleep, great. If not, that's okay. It's just a matter of relaxing my body.

• **READING FOR FUN.** I believe in reading as much as you can. When I need to reenergize or remotivate, Barnes & Noble is a common stop for me. I read every business book I can get my hands on, make some notes, and like magic, I'm refocused. But when it comes to balance and relaxation, I try to read one non-work related book (usually biographies do it for me) every few months. It takes me a while to get through these types of books but it's mostly about putting my mind on something else. They almost act as an escape, something totally unrelated to what I might be dealing with personally or professionally. I've found that if I read a business book before bed, my brain just runs and runs all night long.

- **TEA.** Let me be clear—I'm a coffee person. I have a cup in the morning and a cup after lunch. But in the evenings, to calm down, I'm a tea drinker. There is something calming and soothing for me about drinking a big mug of tea before bed. It starts to put my brain at ease.

- **CLEANING; PUTTING THINGS IN THEIR PLACE.** For me, there is something relaxing and comforting about getting ready for the next day. Setting out my workbag, picking out my clothes, putting some things away around my apartment. It makes me feel like I'm putting things in their place and really bringing the day to a nice close.

- **WALKS.** I just started going on walks in the past few years and I specifically like evening walks right before it gets dark out. I love doing this and feel like it's a great way to wind down. Even if it's by yourself and just around the block. Just a nice quiet walk where you get to go outside, have some time to your thoughts. If it's dark out—bring someone with you!

When you start your first job and try to balance your personal time, you are probably going to get it wrong. And that's okay. This is a big change in your life. You've been studying your whole life just to prepare for this special time. You're inevitably going to get stuck working long hours, ignoring calls from your friends, and eating bagels in the break room. And again, that's okay. We all have our own learning curve. Let the tips throughout this chapter provide some guidance for you as you navigate the waters of your first job. And in case you were wondering: Yes, although it's a crazy time, it's one of the best times of your life. Enjoy yourself.

Epilogue

Dear Reader,

Welcome to the real world. I can't believe our journey together is coming to an end. After reading this book, I hope you understand why I felt the need to write it and fill your mind with tips to help you navigate your work life and your personal life during that first, second, or third job. If even one tip in this book has made you shift the way you think about the real world, I've succeeded in doing my job.

After sharing so many experiences and stories with you, I feel like we're connected. I'm so proud of you. You are going to be so successful, I can feel it through the pages. And my gut tells me our paths will cross again—they always do. Remember, if nothing else, you have a new friend—someone who cares very much about your ability to thrive in whichever career path you've chosen.

I know that you are supposed to live with no regrets. They say to never look back and keep moving forward. Of course, I try my best to do that. However, I can't help but wonder if my life would have been any different had I read this book before entering the real world. I'll never quite know the answer to that but I'm excited to see all of you thrive in your professional careers and adapt to the work-place a little better than I did. Please stay in touch. I'm so honored to be part of your journey. Here's to your real world being the best adventure of your life.

—Lauren Berger

About the Author

LAUREN BERGER is arguably the nation's most in-demand career and internship expert. She is the CEO and founder of the top-internship website www.internqueen.com as well as www.laurenbergerinc.com. Her first book, *All Work, No Pay*, is a national campus bestseller. Berger has been featured on *Today*, *Fox & Friends*, *Marie*, the Hallmark Channel, and other media outlets. She has also appeared in the *New York Times* and *Seventeen*.